D0877628

What Others Are Saying About This Book:

"If you are just starting out and are overwhelmed with the prospect of trying to become a recording artist, this book can serve as an excellent guide as you take your first steps into the real world of the music business."

—Pete Droge

"A great book that teaches the often-ignored basics of a potential career as a recording artist."   —Mike Malinin, The Goo Goo Dolls

"This is the first book you should read if you want to get started today on a career as a recording artist."   —Clay Bergus, Deep Blue Something

"If you want a quick overview of the music business, without all the bull, this is the book to read."   —Lil Troy

"At last, an entertainment attorney offers up the honest truth about becoming a recording artist."   —Bryan Coleman, Union Entertainment Group

DISCARDED From Nashville Public Library

Arm yourself with the information you need to succeed
MUSIC BUSINESS MADE SIMPLE

MUSIC BUSINESS MADE SIMPLE™

A GUIDE TO BECOMING A RECORDING ARTIST

Part of the MUSIC BUSINESS MADE SIMPLE Series

MUSIC BUSINESS MADE SIMPLE™

A GUIDE TO BECOMING A RECORDING ARTIST

by
J.S. Rudsenske

James P. Denk, editor

SCHIRMER TRADE BOOKS
New York/London/Paris/Sydney/Tokyo/Berlin/Copenhagen/Madrid

Schirmer Trade Books
A Division of Music Sales Corporation, New York

Exclusive Distributors:
Music Sales Corporation
257 Park Avenue South, New York, NY 10010 USA
Music Sales Limited
8/9 Firth Street, London W1D 3JB England
Music Sales Pty. Limited
120 Rothschild Street, Rosebery, Sydney, NSW 2018, Australia

Order No. SCH 10135
International Standard Book Number: 0-8256-7295-3

Printed in the United States of America
by Vicks Lithograph and Printing Corporation

Cover Design: Uncle Charlie

Copyright © 2002, 2004 J. Scott Rudsenske and James P. Denk
All rights reserved. No part of this book may be reproduced or transmitted in any form or
by any means, electronic or mechanical, including photocopying, recording, or by any
information storage and retrieval system, without permission in writing from the Publisher.

"Music Business Made Simple" is claimed as a trademark by J S Rudsenske, PLLC.

Learn more about the author at *MusicBusinessMadeSimple.com*

Library of Congress Cataloging-in-Publication Data
Rudsenske, J. Scott, 1963-
  Music business made simple : a guide to becoming a recording artist /
  by J. Scott Rudsenseke ; James P. Denk, editor.— 1st ed.
     p. cm. — (Music business made simple)
  Includes index.
  ISBN 0-8256-7295-3
1. Music trade—Vocational guidance. 2. Popular music—Vocational
guidance. I. Denk, James P. II. Title. III. Series.
ML3790 .R83 2004
780'.23—dc22

2003021455

Dedication
This book is for all the artists who have ever had a dream and just needed a little help in achieving it.

CONTENTS

Acknowledgements

Thanks to Hilary Rudsenske for her unyielding support. A special thank you goes to Doris Lum, Anthony E.P. Hill, and Uncle Charlie for helping with the little things that made this book a reality.

My gratitude certainly goes to Michael Hausman of United Musicians, Pete Droge, Mike Malinin of The Goo Goo Dolls, Clay Bergus of Deep Blue Something, Bryan Coleman of Union Entertainment Group, and Lil Troy. Each read my manuscript during the developmental stage and offered advice and encouragement.

Special thanks go to Jeff Batton, director of marketing, and everyone at *PrintingForLess.com*. This wonderful company helped create a stunning promotional package for this book. (See my discussion of promotional materials in chapter 18, "Creating Your Promotional Package.") *PrintingForLess.com* helped me go all out to create an affordable four-color media kit that included a presentation folder, flyer, postcard, and business card.

Credits

Managing Editor: Andrea M. Rotondo
Developmental Editor: J.P. Denk
Proofreader: Barbara Schultz
Cover Art: Uncle Charlie
Cover Layout: Leonard Hospidor
Production Director: Dan Earley
Interior Design: Len Vogler
Publicity Coordinator: Alison M. Wofford

About the Author

J.S. "Skip" Rudsenske is an entertainment attorney practicing in Houston, Texas. He attended South Texas College of Law and has practiced entertainment law since graduating in 1989. He is licensed in Texas and Tennessee. He is a current and past board member of the Sports and Entertainment Law Section of the Texas Bar. He represents both companies and artists in the music, film, theatrical, and television industries. He also represents successful published authors and visual artists.

Mr. Rudsenske represents national recording artists on Atlantic, MCA, Koch, Priority, Sony, and Universal Records and has been in-house counsel for and represented independent record labels such as Flashpoint International, Wreckshop, Jam Down, and Game Face Records, all distributed through major label distributors. He has represented independent film companies such as Panda Entertainment and Reptile Films.

Over the years, he has personally managed recording artists on independent and major labels. He was the owner of the Urban Art Bar and personally booked and produced events by artists such as Bush, Oasis, Jewel, Jeff Buckley, Creed, Tonic, Matchbox 20, The Goo Goo Dolls, and Better Than Ezra.

His law firm created and maintains the website *MusicBusinessMadeSimple.com*. He is a voting member of NARAS, the organization that presents the Grammy Awards. He is the author of this book and is a regular speaker at music conferences and seminars.

Learn more about Skip at *MusicBusinessMadeSimple.com*.

Photograph by: Lori Brewer

FOREWORD

When I was 15 years old, I played my first professional gig opening for the now-legendary pioneers of the Seattle scene, Malfunkshun. The year was 1984, I was the lead guitarist in a garage band called 25th Hour and we were paid a whopping ten dollars to play a forty-minute set. We could not have been more psyched. We split the money up so that the two guys who drove got three dollars each and the two of us without licenses each got two dollars. The next day I took 50% of my take—a crumpled one dollar bill—and carefully placed it in a small frame and hung it on my bedroom wall. There it was, my first dollar earned in the music business. Many more would follow in the coming years, I hoped.

A few weeks later, my so-called best friend would smash the glass and snatch the bill to buy a can of chewing tobacco. "Is this what lay ahead for me in the music business," I wondered, "getting paid peanuts only to be robbed by people who are supposed to be my friends?"

Of course, this episode did nothing to dull my passion for pursuing a life and career in music. Soon I was writing my own songs, singing, and playing solo acoustic gigs among the clatter, din, and hiss of espresso machines in local coffee shops. Instead of getting paid peanuts, I was getting paid beans… coffee beans. Next, I began playing clubs around Seattle and making demos on a cassette four-track machine and in local studios. I built a loyal following around town, which led to interest from managers, booking agents, critics, and publishers. After a showcase at South By Southwest Music Conference I had offers for recording contracts from several major labels. Since signing my first record deal in 1993, I have made several records and toured extensively. I have enjoyed critical acclaim, the praise of some of my musical heroes, and enough commercial success to stay in the game.

I stumbled into other areas of my career quite by accident. I began producing after recording some "demos" for singer-songwriter Elaine Summers. Pearl Jam's Stone Gossard heard these funky lo-fi gems and released them on his label, Loosegroove. (A few years later he would enlist me to produce his solo debut *Bayleaf*.) My first opportunity to score a feature film came from a chance meeting while waiting to board a plane at Sea-Tac Airport.

As I look back and compare my career path to the advice laid out in Skip's book, I'm impressed with how much they have in common. Skip stresses the importance of artist development (your songwriting skills and performance style); demystifies the demo recording process; shows you how to design promo materials and get media attention; and walks you through the maze of entertainment attorneys, managers, booking agents, and producers. He does not claim to hold a secret key that will open the door to fame and fortune, but rather teaches the importance of setting both short- and long-term goals and the value of being flexible with those goals as your career unfolds.

If you are just starting out and are overwhelmed with the prospect of trying to become a recording artist, this book can serve as an excellent guide as you take your first steps into the real world of the music business. Likewise, if you've been at it a while and are spinning your wheels, it can help you get moving in a new direction.

Listen to your heart, work hard, and be ready when luck comes your way.   —**Pete Droge**

About Pete Droge

As a teenager, Pete Droge saved his money, planning to move to New York City where he could sleep on a relative's couch while pursuing his musical ambitions. Instead, at eighteen he used the money to purchase his first piece of recording equipment. Now, after countless recording projects in his Seattle studio, The Puzzle Tree, it seems clear that a four-track recorder was a far better investment than moving across the country.

Droge's 1994 debut, *Necktie Second*, was hailed as a success and was a definite departure from the grunge that was the norm on the Seattle scene at the time. While touring extensively with Neil Young, Tom Petty, Melissa Etheridge, and Sheryl Crow to promote *Necktie Second* and its follow-up *Find a Door*, Droge's sound began to expand. He gained even more fans and respect from his peers with the release of his third solo album, *Spacey and Shakin.*

After firmly establishing his career as a solo artist, Pete branched out into record production, film scoring, and co-writing. He scored the film *Tatoo: A Love Story* and wrote "Small Town Blues" and performed it in the Cameron Crow blockbuster, *Almost Famous*. He's also been dabbling in a little side project called The Thorns. This new harmony band features Droge and fellow singer/songwriters Matthew Sweet and Shawn Mullins. With a full-length album out in May 2003, tours with the Jayhawks and Dixie Chicks, and piles of press clippings that could reach the moon, The Thorns became an "experiment" turned musical juggernaut.

Even with his participation in The Thorns, Droge still had time to release his fourth full-length solo album, *Skywatching*, in conjunction with United Musicians. His collaborative ideal led him to work with this consortium, home of Aimee Mann, Michael Penn, and Bob Mould. The organization unites musicians and allows them to share resources so their independent careers can flourish.

Critics have always respected Droge's work, with *Rolling Stone* noting, "The strength of Droge's personal conviction emphasizes what is true rather than what is merely tried." Perhaps the *Los Angeles Times* nails that Droge quality best: "Droge writes about the longing and doubts of relationships with the softer, more customized edge of his singer-songwriter heroes, including Dylan, Neil Young, Tom Petty and Gram Parsons."

Learn more about Pete Droge at *PeteDroge.com*.

INTRODUCTION

Who should read this book?

Do you want to become a recording artist? Are you starting up a new band? Are you an established local musician seeking to reach a larger audience? Perhaps you're a successful professional musical artist in need of some solid advice on the music business and the next steps toward even greater success. This book is for you.

The fact is, every serious musician or vocalist needs a little guidance as he or she works to become the best, most successful artist he or she can be. The advice and information in this book applies to every new or developing musician, vocalist or group—regardless of musical style—and also to those who would seek to help these artists early in their musical careers.

Why should you buy this book?

Almost everyone knows someone who has dreamed of stardom. Every year, thousands of people take their shot at a music career. Most do not succeed. Some crash and burn spectacularly. Others simply get tired of playing for pennies and empty chairs. But some *do* succeed. We wonder: "Why did Band A make it big while Band B (who are at least as good) never got beyond the local bar scene?" If you can figure this out, please let me know. You've found the magic formula for which we've been searching.

In fact, there is no formula, and this book does not provide a map to

Easy Street. Success in the music business is a matter of development, hard work, and a little luck.

One definition of luck is "preparation meeting opportunity." This book provides practical information and advice on how to handle issues and problems that arise during your development as an artist. It will help you to prepare and to increase your opportunities in the music industry.

Of course, you will need a lot more than a book to answer all your questions and to get the detailed guidance you'll need as your career advances. For that, you will eventually hire a personal manager and entertainment attorney. But there will be many steps before you get to that point. As they say, you can't go from the mailroom to the boardroom without education and experience. Even if you know nothing about the music business, this book can help you get out of the mailroom and started on your way to a career as a recording artist.

Why did I write this book?

Before you (the musical artist) will need a personal manager or an entertainment attorney, you need questions answered, advice on developing your career, and help in setting goals. I wrote this book to answer questions I get from aspiring artists every day. And while there are many good resources available, I have yet to find a book that provides a user-friendly, step-by-step approach to becoming a recording artist. The information and advice in this book has been tested and proved with the many artists I have advised and represented in my career. No matter what kind of music you make, from hip-hop to honky tonk, this book will help in your development as a successful recording artist.

What qualifies me to give this advice?

I've practiced entertainment law since 1989 and have represented national recording artists, independent record and film companies, and developing local bands. I have also personally managed artists on independent labels. I have owned a 300-seat live music venue and personally booked/produced events by artists such as Bush, Oasis, Old 97s, Jewel, Soul Coughing, Jeff Buckley, Creed, Bob Mould, Tonic, Better Than Ezra, Goo Goo Dolls, The Toadies, Matchbox 20, and others. I have helped to develop artists, and have produced and distributed their records through my own independent record label. I have also taught music business classes at colleges and technical schools. I'm quite sure I don't know everything. But I am sure that my knowledge and experience will be helpful to you. To find out more about my law firm or me, please visit my Web site at www.musicbusinessmadesimple.com.

About the format of the book

This book is organized to follow the steps and stumbling blocks you might encounter from your earliest development to your first record deal. However, you do not have to read this book from start to finish to obtain the information you seek. Each short chapter is intended to stand on its own and provide information about a single subject. This format will allow you to obtain real, common sense answers with the flip of a page.

PART
ONE

GETTING
STARTED

An Overview 1

I wrote this book to provide useful business tips and direction to musicians. In this chapter, I describe some of the most important steps you will take early in the process of obtaining a career in recording and/or live performance.

First, realize that your path and your goals may change over time, and that simply knowing the way doesn't guarantee you'll reach your destination. The level of success you achieve as an artist will be based on many factors. Some factors—such as desire, goals, dedication, and perseverance—you can control. Others—such as musical cycles, circumstances, and just blind luck—are beyond your control.

Even under the best circumstances, the process of building and obtaining a career as a musical artist takes years. Even the few steps described in this chapter can take a couple of years or more to complete. At any point, outside factors might require you to change direction. This definitely doesn't mean you can't reach your ultimate goal. You just need to be prepared to alter your course and adapt to current circumstances.

Your first assignment is to approach a career in the music industry just as you would any other. Maybe the qualifications and rewards are different, but wanting to be "a star" in the music business is not unlike wanting to become a doctor, engineer, fireman, or astronaut. Sure, there are more doctors than music stars, but the paths to these careers are not as different as you might think. To be successful in music—or in any profession—you need education, training, talent, and experience.

Second, you must take the big leap. Yes, it's true. Before you can be a star, you have to build up your talents and learn about music by singing or playing a musical instrument, recording, performing, etc. This is an essential step in your development, and the earlier you begin, the better.

As you practice and learn, you'll come to understand your strengths and weaknesses. Maybe your singing is weak (and scares the cat), but you have a real knack for the guitar. You'll discover a lot during your early efforts, which will help to define your next steps.

Third, after developing some level of skill, you'll want to test your talents by performing live. I discuss performance in depth in chapter 12, "It's All in the Performance." The main thing to know early on is that you should perform as often as possible. Live performance is the best way to perfect your raw musical talents and to present them to your future fans.

This is a great time to gain feedback from fans and critics. Of course, some people have no idea what they're talking about, but you should gladly accept constructive criticism and use it to improve for the next performance. Eventually, your live show will be the most important component of your career development, because it can help you get a deal, gain and keep fans, and make money consistently.

Fourth, when your musical and performance skills have reached the point that your group has performed for a few months without getting booed or thrown off the stage, it's time to record a demonstration recording or "demo." I discuss the details of this process in chapter 15, "Recording Your First Demo."

Making and having a demo will aid your development in two important ways. Naturally, you'll learn something about the recording process, which will become more important as your career advances. Also, you'll have a recording of your material on cassette or CD: A product. Sure, your friends will want copies, and you can sell your demo at live performances. Equally important, you can give your demo to clubs or festival booking agents, local newspaper music reviewers, potential managers, entertainment attorneys, record label executives, or even other musicians with whom you might want to work. But, not all at once! I talk more about when to contact these different people later in the book.

During the entire development process and throughout your career, you will be influenced by certain music and make choices about the kind(s) of music you write and/or perform. This is an important part of your growth as an artist that helps you choose a musical path. Initially, you may choose to write/perform gospel, rhythm & blues, classical, hip-hop, pop, rock, jazz, country, or some combination of genres. I say "initially" because an artist may change his or her preferred musical genre several times over a career. You will also begin to figure out if you want to be a musician, a lead singer, a member of a group, a solo artist, etc.

All of this can change as you continue to develop. It's your career; you're free to follow your own path. It's not unusual for a guitarist to become a lead singer, or for a lead singer to begin playing an instrument, as well. In fact, it's pretty common. This will all be part of finding—and understanding—yourself as an artist.

Fifth, during and after you have taken all these steps, and after you have chosen a musical path that is right for you, you must practice, practice, practice. No matter where you are in your musical career, you will always need to practice. Improve your musical, songwriting, and live performance skills. Record more demos or full-length recordings and prepare to present yourself to the public and—later—record labels.

One common misconception is that major labels develop artists. This is absolutely *not* true. Labels don't hear a talented person and say, "Okay, let's create a look for this guy. Get him a vocal coach, a wardrobe and performance coach, a limo..." This just doesn't happen. You have to bring the whole package, including performance ability, to the major labels. And the way you get this package is by preparing beforehand.

Many artists do this by using time with an independent label to develop their artistry, songwriting, and performance. You may sign with an independent label because your music is not of the commercial variety sought by major labels right now. But your style may eventually become commercial as tastes of the buying public change. Artists like Green Day, Ryan Adams, and Run DMC were not huge successes immediately. But they kept making their music on independent labels and, obviously, they have gone on to enjoy great success. So make your music, learn your craft, and don't worry about selling a million records. Tastes in music do change, and when they do, you'll be ready.

Be an Artist First

In many ways, music is like any career: There's a lot of hard work and a long road to the top. During the tough times (and there will be plenty), you may begin to second-guess your decision to pursue a career in this business. It's hard to feel too excited when you played for an audience of 12 people last night and made $50. Then, after the show, your bassist quit. All the while, your parents keep telling you to get a "real job."

Right about now, you might be asking yourself, "Why am I doing this? Why didn't I go to law school like my parents told me?" First, you didn't go to law school because you don't want to be a lawyer. And the world certainly doesn't need any more lawyers. Sure, it's not always fun or easy to be a musical artist. Usually, there's too much work; not enough pay. Like I said, it's like most other careers.

But as the saying goes, "Do what you love, and the money will follow." I have found this to be true. If you don't have passion for your work, you won't do it well and you'll be unhappy. Whatever your life's calling may be, you'll be most happy if you follow it. So if you're an artist, accept it and be the best artist you can be.

Maybe you've been struggling a long time without a lot of success. You're tired of small audiences and corner-store burritos. Well, life as an artist is not a race. Yes, the music business tends to desire young and attractive artists as pop stars. Artists and repertoire (A&R) people at major labels seem to believe that you're over the hill when you turn twenty-six. Just as most people are beginning their careers, the music industry is saying an artist's career is over.

What can you do about that? Most important, you can try to develop your craft early. It takes five to ten years to develop as a recording artist. If you show exceptional talent at a young age, you may have opportunities with major labels that other artists do not. But if you take longer to develop, your career definitely is not over. It's just following a different path from the careers of some other artists.

Most young artists (sixteen or seventeen years old) gaining attention in the music scene today started down this path at a very early age. Most probably started playing music and performing when they were seven or eight. But if you get started later in life, it's okay. There's no reason to go through life frustrated by the fact that you did not start your musical career in kindergarten. How many people do you know who started preparing for their careers at that age?

Whether 5 or 15 or 25 or 55, you're an artist. You can't turn back time; you can only move forward. You may not have chosen your starting point, but you can have a big influence over where you finish. And isn't that the most important issue? Once you accept this, you can expend your energy on becoming a successful artist.

Some artists develop more quickly and appear on TV more frequently than others. They get paid more than $39 and two beers for their gigs. They're on major labels. Maybe they have more opportunities, resources, and connections than the rest of us. You can't control that.

Other artists are on independent labels. They drive a van from show to show for $200 each night. No roadies, no fancy dressing rooms, no television crews. And hey, some artists are not on any label at all. None of these artists is more successful than another (unless you measure success merely by the size of the paycheck and number of television appearances). It just means they are different. They all could be equally happy and consider themselves successful.

What about you? Maybe you perform once a week at the local coffeehouse for $20 a night. Here's a news flash: You are no less an artist than the people you see on TV. Do what you love, and I promise your time will come. It may not be tomorrow. It may not be next year. But if you hang in there, your time will come. I'm not promising limos, shrieking groupies, and stadium tours. But you will have success. Be an artist first, and the success will follow.

Things You Can Do Today To Build Your Career
1) Accept that you're an artist and embrace the calling.
2) Define what artistic success means to you.
3) There is no promise of fame or fortune, but with talent, hard work, and a little luck, you can make a living as a musical artist.

This Is A 3 Career

You have to treat a professional music career like any other. In addition to talent, it requires a lot of hard work and discipline. Your friends and family may consider you a genius prodigy, and maybe you are. But even prodigies must educate themselves and obtain experiences to improve and grow as artists. You can't go from the coffeehouse to Madison Square Garden in one day, or even one year.

Like all careers, this one starts with education, such as vocal or musical instrument lessons. It certainly requires practice and/or recitals. But take comfort: Your friends and family will suffer with you while you learn to sing or play your chosen instrument. This is all part of the development process. Along the way, you'll discover that your effort, dedication, and perseverance can produce rewards.

Like most professionals, artists must take on different jobs to gain experience and get promoted. For instance, a professional accountant (say, someone to handle your multitrillion-dollar contract from Sony Music) might change jobs and/or companies to get more or different experience. This accountant will learn what he or she likes and does not like in the field of accounting, and may change direction to follow his or her preferred path.

Your musical career will probably be much the same. No matter where or how it begins, your own style, talents, and interests will emerge over time. As you develop, you'll gain new experiences and skills. You will learn from, and be influenced by, those around you. All of this will affect the music you make.

Most likely, you will work with many other musical artists. I assure you, no singer or musician stays with the same group throughout his or her career. It's not always easy to move on, but it is natural. Most artists will go through many groups or bands as they develop musical tastes, artistic differences, and personal relationships. You need these experiences to find the right career path, the best musicians to work with, and your own musical style.

It is easy to follow the development of most careers: High school, college, maybe an advanced degree. You land that first job and feel excited for a week. Then, things start to get boring. Maybe you don't like your boss. You become dissatisfied and unfulfilled just as you begin the long haul up that "corporate ladder."

Some people choose a less structured approach. They advance their careers with experience instead of higher education. As an artist, you can take the same approach. You can learn from educational institutions, from private institutions, or from teaching yourself and "just doing it." There is no wrong way, just different paths and styles.

In any case, treat the process of growth and advancement the same way people do in any other career. Understand that you will have to change jobs, relocate, learn new skills and procedures, make mistakes, and earn a living while figuring out exactly what direction you wish to take. All of this is part of the experience of any career.

Things You Can Do Today To Build Your Career
1) Get educated about the business. *(See the Resource section at the back of this book for leads on good books, magazines, and music conferences.)*
2) Practice your craft. Pledge to devote an hour or more a day to becoming a better musician.
3) Consider music school or on-the-job training by working in a nightclub or being a performing cast member at a local theater company or theme park.

LEARN FROM 4 OTHER ARTISTS

One of the best ways to learn about artist development and the music business is to study the steps successful artists have taken to reach their goals. Very likely, these artists went through many of the same things that you will experience. It is better to learn from their mistakes than to repeat those missteps yourself. Eliminating the dreaded process of trial and error, and avoiding the problems others have had when they were in your situation, will help to speed your trip to success.

One useful and enjoyable resource is the *Behind the Music* series on VH1. This program provides the now-familiar, in-depth studies of the rise and fall (and usually, second rise) of the featured artist. You can learn a lot about all the hard work, mistakes, and small successes that have shaped these artists' careers.

It's also helpful to read or listen to interviews with successful artists. A good interview will cover the artist's rise to fame and usually will include stories about things the artist did early on that contributed to later success. As you watch, read, listen, and learn, you may recognize some common themes among the different stories, regardless of the artists' musical styles. One of my favorite magazines for stories about musical artists in Uncut, published in the U.K.

Another way to learn about an artist's development is to purchase books about that artist. *(See the Resource section at the back of this book for sug-*

gestions.) Most established musical artists, the people who influence the work of today's stars, have been written about. One extremely informative book about the development of the music business and record industry is *Mansion on the Hill* by Fred Goodman. This book tracks the growth of the music industry through the 1970s by following the careers of several key figures, including Bruce Springsteen, Neil Young, the Eagles, and David Geffen.

While there is no one formula for making it in the music industry, you can do some simple things to increase your chances for success. One of these is to learn as much as possible about the business and those who have enjoyed success within it. Strategies and practices that have helped other musical artists attain success may help you, too. And knowing the mistakes of others may help you to avoid repeating them. In both ways, you can help speed up your own development as a musical artist.

Things You Can Do Today To Build Your Career
1) Buy or rent videos/DVDs of live musical performances and critique them. What works? What doesn't? What elements can you "borrow" for your own performances?
2) Watch televised biographies of musicians and pay careful attention to their stories about breaking into the business. Is there any advice or experience that can be helpful to you now?
3) Read books and magazines about music and musicians. *(See the Resource section at the back of this book for suggestions.)*

LEARN ABOUT 5 THE BUSINESS

I receive many e-mails, letters, and telephone calls from people asking me to explain what I know about the music business. Unfortunately, there is no way I can do this in a short period of time. Even if I could, my lecture wouldn't be very beneficial to even the most attentive student, because it's too much information to digest in one sitting. It takes time for it all to sink in.

Though I have been practicing law in the entertainment industry since 1989, I never stop learning about this business. I learn in two ways. First, I continue to study books and articles about the music business and the law. I also attend legal seminars and music conferences each year to learn about the most recent changes in, and interpretations of, music law, and to discuss legal and business issues with other entertainment attorneys and industry professionals.

As a musical artist, it isn't necessary for you to become an expert, but for your own protection, you should definitely learn about the music business. The further your career advances, the more you need to know. There are numerous information sources. Other than this book, there are several basic books on the music business. Don't buy the biggest, most detailed, and most expensive book. It might look impressive on your coffee table, but it won't teach you much. In fact, it will be intimidating and complicated to read, and you will end up using it as a coffee table.

Instead, buy books that are the smallest and easiest to read, like this one. Even if you think you have experience in the music business, a simple resource can always teach you something new or reinforce what you already know. Stick with solid, user-friendly resources that help you to become a better artist and to maneuver through the fundamental issues of the music business. Search your local or favorite online bookstore.

Learning the basics will help you to understand the business and have realistic expectations. Many artists make decisions based on misinformation. Unfortunately, their lack of understanding and false expectations make it very difficult for these artists to move their careers forward.

Knowing the fundamentals of contracting for gigs, or of negotiating/ signing a record or management deal will help you recognize legitimate deals (*and* bad ones). It won't eliminate mistakes altogether, but it will help you make better choices when opportunities (or potential disasters) arise. You don't have to know everything, but you should know enough to spot potential problems. When something important does arise, or when you're not sure how to proceed, you should seek the professional advice of an entertainment attorney or other music-business professional.

One excellent place to obtain solid, current information is at a music-business seminar or music conference. The various panels and discussions at these events allow you to gain different perspectives on music-industry issues from professionals in a variety of fields within the music industry. I talk more about this in chapter 20, "Music Conferences."

The music business is always changing. Learn as much as you can, and do your best to keep up with current issues. Once you know the basics, you'll be able to understand how and why the business is changing. As they say, information is power. Being informed about the music business gives you the power to move your career forward more quickly.

Things You Can Do Today To Build Your Career
1) Accept that you will need to learn continually about the music business.
2) Build a library of easy-to-understand resources about the business to use as references until you are able to hire a manager, entertainment attorney, booking agent, etc.
3) Attend a music conference and start learning and networking. (*See the Resource section in the back of this book for a list of music conferences.*)

IMPORTANCE OF SETTING GOALS

*E*veryone has dreams: Things they want to accomplish. For some, that vision includes life as a professional recording artist. Since you're reading this book, maybe this is your dream, too. No matter what your ultimate destination may be, a series of objective, attainable goals will help you get there.

Why is it important to set goals? Because it gives you a plan of action. If your ultimate goal is to become a successful musical recording artist, you will need short-term goals along the way to help you get there.

Before you begin this process, understand that your goals may change and become more specific as you gain more experience and develop as an artist. This is completely normal. Simply knowing that your goals may change will keep you from becoming frustrated if you don't achieve the goals you set at the very beginning of your journey. As you grow and evolve artistically and personally, you will revise and reassess your professional goals, as well.

So, how do you go about setting goals? First, get a pencil (with an eraser) and a pad of paper. Brainstorm. Just say any goal that comes to mind and write it down. Don't evaluate, just write. At this point, no goal is unrealistic. You will review and revise your list later (thus the eraser). Maybe you'll never win a Grammy, headline a stadium tour, or date a supermodel. (Then again, maybe you will.) But for the moment, allow yourself to dream.

This helps you visualize what you want. If you can't say or see a goal, you can't achieve it. Keep your list somewhere handy so you can refer back to it on occasion, write new goals, and change old ones.

Your first goal will be the ultimate destination you want to reach. Start with a broad goal, and keep in mind that it is likely to change during your career. Your ultimate goal might be to become a successful recording artist, live concert pianist, or rock guitarist. Other long-term goals might include having a successful national tour or creating a new genre of music.

Once you decide on your long-term destination, you need to set a series of short-term goals to help you get there. The next chapter will help show you how.

Things You Can Do Today To Build Your Career
1) Begin setting goals for your future in the music business. It will help you determine what's important to you.
2) Accept that the goals you make a priority today may shift as your career progresses.
3) Brainstorm several broad, long-term goals. Be as specific as possible and don't be afraid to aim high. Just remember, the big goals will probably take longer to reach.

SETTING SHORT-TERM GOALS

Setting short-term goals is essential to achieving your long-term goals. One example of a short-term goal will be to learn how to play an instrument. (This same thought process is applied to become a singer). Maybe you want to play several instruments. Great! Multitalented musicians certainly have more options. But still, your first short-term goal is to learn to play one of the instruments.

After you decide on an instrument, obviously, you have to obtain that instrument. If you don't have a music store nearby, maybe you have a pawnshop that sells instruments. Or check the classified section of your local newspaper.

Once you have your instrument of choice, your immediate goal will be to learn how to play it. If you are in high school, you may have the opportunity to learn to play in the school band. If your school band does not use the instrument you want to play, or you do not have a school band, or it's too late to begin playing in the school band, you have to devise a different plan to learn the instrument.

You can take private lessons with a teacher or enroll in a class at a local educational facility. If you don't have money for this, teach yourself with how-to books, videos and DVDs, and songbooks. *(See the Resources section at the back of this book for some suggestions.)* And if you're *really* broke, you can check these materials out from the library.

After you begin to develop your musical skills, you will need new short-term goals: To be the best in your high school band or choir, to win a music contest, etc. After high school, you may decide to go to a college to pursue a path in concert or choral music. All the while, you can also develop your skills in an outside band or group.

As you gain experience and progress even further as a performing artist, you will continue to develop more and more ambitious goals. These might include building a fan base in each city in your region, creating a series of independent records, and getting your records played on the radio.

You get the idea. It is important to set short-term goals—or stepping stones—along the path to your ultimate destination, rather than take one giant leap, only to fall. Small successes will help keep you motivated and moving toward your long-term goal(s).

Right now, you probably don't have enough experience in the music business to set all your goals. Don't be discouraged. You may just need help. Excellent resources include experienced professionals in the industry (if you know any), and books and articles about successful recording artists or the music industry in general. You can always revise your goals as you learn more.

And remember, there is no right or wrong strategy to achieve your goals. Two artists can take completely different paths to reach the same destination. Only you can decide what is best for you, based on your circumstances and resources as you progress. Today, your main goal is to get pointed in the right direction and get moving.

Things You Can Do Today To Build Your Career
1) Break down your long-term goals and list several short-term steps that will help you achieve them. These steps are your short-term goals.
2) Commit to working toward at least one of your short-term goals every day.
3) Continually revisit your goals and brainstorm new short-term steps that will help you achieve them.

REASSESSING AND CHANGING YOUR GOALS

You might not achieve all your goals as you progress in your musical career. This doesn't mean you failed. Most likely, you simply changed what you ultimately wanted or set more realistic goals, based on your experiences. The beauty of setting goals is that you can reassess and set new ones whenever necessary. You should always be open to this possibility.

Perhaps, in the beginning, you started with the ultimate goal of being a successful recording artist who plays piano. At that time, you also set the specific goal of becoming a pop star. While pursuing pop stardom, you perfect your piano playing and songwriting skills, and make a career out of performing music. For reasons far beyond your control, you don't become a pop star.

However, over the years, you write many songs that become big hits for other artists. This makes you a lot of money, and helps these artists' careers. The public may not know you, but these artists do. At the worst, you end up with some cool friends and a mountain of royalties. Not bad.

Eventually, you have written so many hit songs for others that you decide to record your own versions of these songs. All those grateful artists agree to perform on your record, so you have the best backing band in the world. Of course, your record sells a million copies, the public gains a whole new appreciation for your music, and you take home that Grammy after all. So while you did not achieve "pop stardom" you did reach your goal of becoming a very successful recording artist who plays piano.

Obviously, things usually don't work out quite *that* well. The point is, although you might never become the King or Queen of Pop, you can achieve success as a recording artist in other ways. When you realize that you may not achieve one or more of your goals, you have two choices: Quit or reassess your goals and keep moving forward. If you have a passion for your art and are committed to this career, you will find a way to make it work.

Reassessment is often difficult for artists as they go through their careers. But music is like any career. You cannot map out every detail of your future in this business. Sometimes you have to make a hard assessment and act accordingly. This applies to any career. Instead of being frustrated by the process, embrace it and be prepared. When things seem to be going badly, or you're not sure of which direction to take, honest reassessment and strong action (often with the help of other industry professionals) can turn your career around and lead you toward the success you've always envisioned.

Things You Can Do Today To Build Your Career
   1) Reassess your goals periodically and determine if they are still relevant.
   2) Brainstorm for new goals, as needed.
   3) Follow your passion for music as you reassess your goals.

PART
TWO

DEVELOPMENT

YOUR FIRST STEP

*A*s someone said, a long time ago, before they had cars, or even mopeds, "a journey of a thousand miles begins with one step." There are many things you will need to do and learn as you develop as a singer or musician. The first step is simply to begin the journey. Often, this step is the most difficult. But you can't be an artist sitting on your couch. You have to jump in there, learn to play the instrument, and/or sing on key.

Of course, if you want to sing, you don't have to buy an instrument. But if you want to play guitar, keyboards, trumpet, or whatever, well, you need to purchase your chosen instrument. It doesn't have to be expensive. You might find an old guitar at a garage sale, negotiate a deal on a used Yamaha acoustic at your local music store, or borrow a guitar from a friend.

After you have an instrument, you'll probably need to take lessons. This also does not have to be expensive. To get started, you can even buy a "how-to" book or video. Eventually, to really hone your skills, you'll need to call upon some experts to provide individual instruction. Don't be fooled. No matter how much you develop on your own, you need the experts.

Think about tennis pros. Even the very top players in the world have coaches. I hope you become one of the top musical artists in the world, too. But even if that happens, you will always benefit from the right person's insight, motivation, and instruction.

The professional music business, like other entertainment industries, has its occasional prodigy. Some people are so gifted that they bypass all the preliminary junk and head straight for stardom. They are part of a very, very select group who are not required to do many of the things I discuss in this book.

Maybe you're one of these musical geniuses, but you're probably not. If you *are* a prodigy, there still are no guarantees. It just means you'll have fewer hurdles to clear, which will allow you to move your career forward a little sooner than everyone else.

If you're like the other 99.9% of us, you're going to have to work to build a career. But take encouragement from the fact that 99.9% of all successful musical artists followed the same path you will: Development, hard work, and persistence. With these qualities, everyone has a chance to become a professional musical artist.

Once you can play most of the notes on an instrument and have learned all the songs in your songbook, move on. Learn to play or sing new songs. Practice playing or singing the notes more clearly. This repetition may not be much fun. In fact, it might be downright painful. But you have to "build your chops" so you can take the next step and perform in front of people. Sing or play in your church, to friends and family, or at school. Take every opportunity to perfect your craft. This desire to improve should drive you for the rest of your career.

And remember, no matter how good you think you are, you can learn from others. I am always impressed when I hear musical artists compliment other artists' playing or singing ability. And it is very interesting when a guitarist, for instance, tells me that he saw someone pull off a cool maneuver or riff during a show, and that he wants to incorporate it into his own performance. Never stop learning, and never start to believe you are so good that you can't learn something from a teacher or another artist.

Things You Can Do Today To Build Your Career
1) Just do it. Your journey begins with the first step. Have the courage to go for it.
2) Do one thing to advance your career *today* and *every* day: Practice, meet another local musician, talk with a club owner about getting on an upcoming bill, etc.
3) Realize that it will be a long road and you've got much to learn along the way to achieving your goals.

PRACTICE, PRACTICE, PRACTICE

How do you get to Carnegie Hall? A: Practice, practice, practice! Sure, it's the oldest joke in the entertainment industry. I'm not sure it ever was actually funny, but it does make a point. Nothing is more important to your success than practice. If you want to reach your maximum potential as a musician, you *must* practice. A lot. *Until it hurts.* It's as simple as that.

There is no substitute for hard work. And there is no feeling like the one you'll get when you see all your hard work pay off. No one will ever know how many thousand hours you put in, or how many sacrifices you made to develop your skills. It's lonely and it's not glamorous. But practice separates the artists from the wanna-be's. Which one are you?

Many people are born with talent. A lot of them have more talent than you or me. But talent is only one part of the equation. You also have to have the desire. It's a fact: A moderately talented artist with a real passion for his or her craft will enjoy quicker and greater success than a hugely talented, but unmotivated artist. You must have both talent and desire to succeed.

Seek out the different options available for you to hone your skills. Some artists begin with music lessons in school or from private teachers. Some begin in the high-school marching band and go on to study music or choral performance in college. Many artists take private lessons. No way is better than the others. Some options present a beginner with an organized, disciplined, and scheduled system for practicing and performing. Others are more flexible, but require greater discipline on your part. As you develop your musical skills and interests, you will decide which suit you best.

The only "rule" is that you can never stop practicing or working on your craft. Even if you become the best in the world at what you do, it still requires persistence, discipline, and passion to do it every day. And no matter what, you will always need to work on fundamentals, write new songs, or rehearse performances. Even professional athletes practice every day, with the coach emphasizing execution of fundamental principles. The same is true for musical artists. Sometimes, professionals—in all fields—get lazy and forget the basics. But to be your best, you have to practice "the boring stuff." Focus on developing a strong command of the fundamentals, and never be afraid to take a lesson or get a new perspective from a teacher or fellow musician.

Things You Can Do Today To Build Your Career
1) Practice on your own, with your band, or with other local musicians.
2) Develop a strong command of the fundamentals.
3) Take lessons, even if you think you don't need them.

Gotta Have Great Songs 11

You're beginning to see that there is no magic formula for success in the music business. But there are some things—such as developing excellent live performance skills—that you can do to increase your chances of making it. What else do you need? If anything is as important as a strong live performance, it's great songs. You *must* have great songs. It might sound simple, but it isn't.

Lots of people can come up with a ditty; very few can write a really good song. This is one place where you can set yourself apart and earn your reputation as a musical artist. It's a gift that requires talent, practice, and usually some study. I encourage you to utilize all the books, classes, lessons, and other resources available to help you develop this art.

You may get noticed with your playing or singing skills, but record labels are looking for exceptional songs (and don't forget the live performance) to go with that talent. They will not help you find songs. They do not sign musicians—even very talented ones—with boring tunes.

When you approach a label, you need to impress them with your songs. It's okay if you don't write your own music, but don't put a cover song (a popular radio song recorded by a known recording artist) on your demo. Instead, work with a professional songwriter (and learn from him/her); be the first to record the song(s) you submit. Even if you didn't write them, the songs need to be "yours." And they need to be great.

So what makes a great song? Well, I've never written one, so I can't tell you how to do it. And because music is subjective, everyone has a different opinion about what is good. But regardless of the public's musical taste or the style of your music, you absolutely must have strong songs to achieve success in this business.

A good way to practice the craft of songwriting is to attend a writing workshop or seminar. Many of the performing rights organizations, such as ASCAP (American Society of Composers, Authors, and Publishers), BMI (Broadcast Music, Inc.), and SESAC (Society of European Stage Authors and Composers) offer workshops for members and non-members, alike. (*See the Resource section in the back of this book for more information on performing rights organizations.*)

A professional songwriter, who wrote several hits, once told me that part of the trick is writing about something that everyone can relate to, but saying it in a way that has never been said before. Also, a song has to be memorable. It has to make people *feel* something. Whether through words, or music, or (most likely) a combination of both, a great song evokes a response. You remember it and want to hear it over and over, to get that feeling again. So you buy the record. And that's what's most important to record labels. They know great songs sell records.

It is difficult for many artists to be objective about the quality of their songs. This is understandable. So as you write, it is critical to get feedback from objective people who listen to your music and songs. When I say "objective," I mean people other than family and friends. Listeners who will be critical, fair, and honest, pointing out strengths and weaknesses.

Your family and friends are a fine start for encouragement, but eventually you'll have to leap into the forum of public opinion, playing your songs for live audiences. If your songs continue to get a good response from strangers—lots of strangers—you probably are beginning to write good stuff.

Things You Can Do Today To Build Your Career
  1) Study popular songs and break them down into their components. What elements do they all share? What's different? Can you incorporate these elements into your songs?
  2) Attend a songwriting workshop.
  3) Join a performing rights association such as ASCAP, BMI, or SESAC, and read applicable magazines such as *Performing Songwriter*. (*See the Resource section in the back of this book for more information.*)

IT'S ALL IN THE PERFORMANCE

12

There's no way to guarantee success in the music industry. I haven't found any secret pathway to stardom, and I can't promise that you'll achieve all your goals. But I *can* tell you the single most important factor (or at least one of the top three) in obtaining a record deal and enjoying a long career as a musical artist. Nope, it's not a stylish photo, a glowing concert review in the newspaper, a great recording—maybe not even great songs. Those components are very important and they definitely can help to get, and keep, a label's attention. But as I will remind you later, it's your live performance that will usually make or break the deal.

You can be born as a child prodigy musician, hire the best producer in the world, and take vocal lessons for 20 years. But without a dynamite live performance, you won't get a call back from potential managers, labels, booking agents, etc.

You have only one chance to make a first impression. This is not to say that you'll get only one chance to make it in the music business. In fact, you may have multiple opportunities at different stages. However, if you don't have a great performance when you showcase your talent to industry professionals, you'll have a difficult time arousing their excitement a second time.

If someone experienced in the business has read or heard great things about your live performance, he or she will usually want to see you more than once... but only if he or she has heard about you from credible sources. This is why you will include press clippings from known, respected sources in your promotional package (which I talk about later). In the next chapter, I discuss a basic approach to putting together your performance. But before you begin, it is important to know why your live show is so vital.

First, recognize that there are thousands of artists, some with more talent than you, trying to make it in the music business. Second, know that talent plays only a limited roll in your success or marketability as an artist. I know, "marketing" is an ugly word that many musicians believe poisons the artistry of their craft. But you should not equate marketability with commercial success. This simply is not the case.

Here's a new definition that applies to artists in all musical genres. "Marketability" is your ability to inform a potential audience about your music and to get your music to people who like (or might like) your music. Not coincidentally, before offering a contract, a record label will want to determine if the people who buy their records will like your music. Record companies (both big and small) are in business to sell records, and they won't sign you if they don't think you'll make money for them. It's the hard, cold truth. Accept it now. Move on.

One of the best ways (I don't know a better one) to market yourself to record companies, attract an audience, *and* make money is to entertain the buying public. I'm not suggesting you turn to overt commercialization like you hear in so much music on the radio. You don't have to create a Vaudeville act with fire-eaters, dancing girls, and ten costume changes. I'm simply talking about the ability to put on a solid, entertaining live show, regardless of your musical or performance style. Without that, you won't have an audience, a record contract, or a career in music.

Even the youngest bands understand this basic principle: Bring people into the venue and keep their attention. The audience pays to see your performance. They cheer for you, share their energy, and generally make it a lot more fun for you to be onstage. They also purchase refreshments from the venue and buy your demo recordings and T-shirts. Because you've made money for the venue (not to mention for yourself), you get asked back for more shows. That's the way it works.

Record labels also know the power of performance to increase their sales. They understand that a strong live performance can persuade the public to purchase your records now and in the future. This is why your performance ability will be a major factor, if not *the* major factor when and if you are considered by a label. If your performance doesn't translate to the public and industry professionals, then you will not command the attention of either.

Things You Can Do Today To Build Your Career
1) Create your stage persona. Will you be stoic and mysterious? Funny and warm? Passionate and sexy? Work to incorporate those traits into your live shows.
2) Ask club-goers and fans what they liked—and didn't—about your show. Learn from their constructive comments.
3) Forge strong relationships with club/venue owners and ask for their advice. After all, they've seen thousands of bands onstage and can tell you what works and what doesn't.

BEFORE YOU STEP ONSTAGE

Throughout this book, I will continue to remind you of the importance of your live performance. There are professionals who can help you in this area and, as always, I recommend that you rely upon their knowledge and experience. But before you get to that point, here are some steps you can take on your own.

First, rent, borrow from the library, or purchase live concert videos of artists whose music is similar to yours. Watch how they present themselves onstage. Styles of performance have been passed down through musical generations, and there is nothing wrong with learning by mimicking an artist you admire. How many of today's young singers have stolen a move or two from Mick Jagger, Steven Tyler, Michael or Janet Jackson, or James Brown? Look back at heavy metal bands of the 1980s, or watch hip-hop and pop artists today. You can see similar performance styles and movements among artists who perform similar genres of music. Of course, you have to develop your own style, and this will happen naturally over time. But studying the performances of artists in your genre will give you an idea of what appeals to fans who might like your music, too.

Over many years as a band manager, record label owner, and attorney to professional recording artists, I have seen the stage shows of hundreds of bands and artists on major labels. In the process, I observed some things that make their performances run smoothly (or not). With those things in mind, I have generated a simple formula to help you develop and perfect your live performance.

Your first objective as a performing artist is to put together what I call an "A" set. This set includes your best songs, placed in an order that will produce the best live performance. It will not necessarily be the same order as the songs on your album (if you have one). In fact, including songs in your set that are not on the CD, such as cover songs (in your own style), can be a plus. As artists I have worked with will tell you, a lot of thought goes into this "A" set.

Your live performance should be designed to entertain your audience and woo potential record label representatives. When you first begin playing live, your "A" set might only be twenty-five or thirty minutes. This is fine. Your first gigs will probably be opening slots, playing before more established acts. Chances are, the venue will allow you only thirty or forty minutes to play anyway. Just make sure those thirty minutes leave a good impression.

Ultimately, you want to have a forty-five- to sixty-minute set. But don't feel like you have to play every song you've written just to fill time. It's always better to leave the audience wanting more than to play too long. The venue and the bands waiting to play after you will also appreciate your awareness of time. Naturally, as you write more songs or add a cover song or two, you will change the order of the songs, always attempting to find that perfect "A" set.

Some artists will make a set list ten minutes before the show. This is a mistake. It often turns their opportunity to shine into a disjointed presentation of songs. Your live performance is much more than that. No matter how far you rise in the musical world, you always want to be prepared. This is especially important early in your career. When you rehearse for a gig, play songs in the same order as your "A" set. This will help you get a feel for the length or your set, and improve your transition from song to song.

Things You Can Do Today To Build Your Career
1) Go to a lot of live shows or rent concert videos. Pay particular attention to artists who perform the same musical genre you do. What are the highlights of their live set? What's the pacing of the set? What can you apply to your live show?
2) Create an "A" set list of twenty-five to thirty minutes of your best material. Concentrate on the pacing and flow of one song to the next.
3) Grow your "A" set list to forty-five to sixty minutes.

A Formula For Performing

14

After you have a great "A" set, you can concentrate on the energy and dynamics you put into each performance. Below are some things you can do immediately to improve your performance and increase your professionalism.

1. Create a song order that will take your audience on a ride with your best songs. Go with quality over quantity.

2. Rehearse and calculate all stage chatter. Always know what you are going to say and when you're going to say it. And keep it to a minimum! Onstage banter just limits the time you have to play your music. Unless you're performing on VH1's "Storytellers" show, people generally aren't there to hear you talk.

3. All of your instruments should be tuned and in place before you take the stage. At show time, take your positions, greet the audience, tell them who you are, and possibly announce the name of your first song. Then get going! People want to hear you play, not watch you tune your guitar or offer your philosophy on life.

4. Divide your set into sections. Start with three to four solid songs that

work well together and can flow or segue, one into the next. Play these first few songs without any significant break, other than possibly to announce the name of the next song (but, I repeat, less talk is better). This will give the audience a chance to get into your set without disruption or distraction. And once you have their attention, don't let it go.

5. When you're building a set list, consider any instrument changes or major breaks that will occur between songs. Build these breaks into the middle of your set, after the audience has become engaged in your performance. A little creativity—such as including acoustic or *a cappella* songs, a simple but interesting instrument change by one of the players, or some other twist—can be a good thing.

    But beware, any stoppage of play can be a show killer, especially when you are just beginning and are trying to build a fan base. If your changes require too much time, leave them out until you become more established. The audience will be more patient with you then.

    No matter what, keep breaks as brief as possible and rehearse them beforehand so everyone knows exactly what they're supposed to do onstage. Use the time during the break to announce the group's name again and possibly give some other quick information (for example, about upcoming gigs you might have).

6. Your last two songs should be two of your strongest, and they should flow together to make a great finish. Before you play them, tell the audience these are your last two songs and thank the crowd for coming to see you. After the last song, announce your group's name again, wish everyone a good night, and announce any merchandise or CDs you may have for sale after the show. Then, pack up and get offstage so the next band (if there is one) can set up.

7. During a performance, each band member should establish an area onstage and stay within it. Energy and movement are great, but a lot of beginning performers take this too far and create a sense of confusion. I suggest that you imagine an invisible box around your area onstage and not stray too far from that box. Even the lead singer should not enter other band members' space.

8. I encourage vocalists—at least at the beginning—to keep the microphone on the stand and use hand gestures and facial expressions to communicate visually with the audience. Many artists may hold the

microphone, but this style takes work, practice, and in some cases, professional coaching. If you're not very experienced, taking the microphone off the stand can make it look like you are hiding behind it, or are nervous or stiff. The main thing is to connect with the audience by looking at them and performing to them, not for them.

9. Never do an encore. Until you're playing theaters and arenas, it's just not appropriate. Like I said, play two really strong songs to close your set and get offstage. Leave them wanting more.

10. No matter what happens onstage, *never* show the audience that you are bothered, or that something is going wrong. Many artists will call attention to their mistakes, or to technical problems by making sour faces or showing frustration. Most times, the audience will have no idea that anything is wrong. There's no need to tell them. Part of being professional is working through the rough moments calmly. As the saying goes, "Never let them see you sweat."

11. Finally, everything you do onstage should be calculated, planned, and rehearsed, from the set list to instrument changes and even what you are going to say to the crowd at a given point in your performance. You don't need a script, but decide beforehand what you may say to entertain the crowd and communicate with them. This all should be part of your smooth performance.

These guidelines have been proven over time, with many bands, and under different circumstances. Obviously, you will need to adapt them to your own style, but they should provide a solid guide as you begin to develop your performance. Use them in rehearsal so they feel and appear natural during your live show. The key is working on your performance and putting some thought into what you're going to do onstage. Your effort and preparation will definitely show.

Things You Can Do Today To Build Your Career
1) Use rehearsal time to prepare exactly what you will do onstage.
2) Rehearse the show over and over until it's perfect.
3) Immediately after your performance, do a self-critique for things to work on in rehearsal, such as song order, crowd response to songs, instrument changes, etc.

Recording Your First Demo

The term "demo" is an abbreviation for "demonstration." A "demo recording" or "demo" is a recording of three to five songs that is usually less than fully produced. Its purpose is not to be played on the radio, but to demonstrate your talents to various gatekeepers in the music business (club booking agents, media, record labels, etc.) who can help advance your development.

You can record a demo at any time. You can make a demo tape in your rehearsal space on a stereo tape recorder before you ever step into a professional studio. You can record your first live performance. Your skills as a recording engineer, along with the quality of the songs and your performance of those songs, will dictate who you give these tapes to. No matter what, it can be very useful for your development and your creative process to record as much and often as possible.

Naturally, you won't send your home-recorded demo to a record company, but you might give it to the engineer at the studio you use. This will allow the engineer to gain some familiarity with your songs and style, which can save time in the studio. Usually, you'll give your early demos to club booking agents, music festival coordinators, and/or concert promoters to get shows. These professionals will want to get some idea of what you sound like (will your music be interesting to the audience they expect?) and determine if you have a reasonable level of performance talent. Later, you will create much higher-quality demos that you can send to record labels.

For your first demos, I suggest using a small, inexpensive studio—anything from a "garage" or "home" studio to the smallest room at a local recording facility. The objective at this point is to gain experience in a recording session with a studio engineer who will use equipment that is at least a little better than you might own yourself. Of course, you also want to end up with a decent-sounding, mixed (multitrack) recording that represents your talents in a positive way.

Because the recording process is an important part of your development as a musical artist, I suggest you pick several small studios and record a different song at each one. This will help you to determine which studio you like best, which studio makes you sound the best, and where you want to record a complete demo next time. Before making a final decision about spending a lot of money at any studio, try to visit them and listen to some of the work they have done.

After you have recorded a few songs at different studios, you can compile the songs to make your demo, or use your favorite studio to re-record all the songs you recorded at other places. This is a relatively inexpensive way to educate yourself about how things work in the studio, how to get the sound you want, and which studios and engineers you might want to work with in the future. It is also a great way to obtain some recording experience (including mistakes) that will help you learn how to get the best recordings of your songs.

Recording one song at a time at different studios also allows you to record as your schedule and budget allow, without having to book a large, expensive block of time at any one place. Plan on spending about $200 to $400 per recording session. You should be able to record and mix a demo song during one session.

No matter what strategy you use, stay focused while you are recording. It's easy to become overwhelmed and excited when you first get into the studio. Have fun, but remember, you're there to do a job. And it's your money.

On the other hand, recognize that your demo does not have to be radio-quality. Many musicians lose sight of their purpose and spend far too much time and money on a demo, only to regret it when they realize the final product is very simple and often mediocre. You want it to sound as good as it can, but at this point, it certainly doesn't have to be professional-grade.

Here's another important point. Once you have worked out a deal with a studio, don't let the owner or engineer talk you into spending more money and time than you planned. It's important that you can trust the studio to work within your time and budget to make the best recording possible. Most are honest, but some will try to take advantage of your inexperience. That is another reason why it's important to shop around and record one or two songs with different studios. You'll get an idea of how well they record your songs, and you'll get a feel for the people working there.

And what do you do with your demo after it's finished? Well, your mom and friends might like a copy. More important, you will give your demo to owners or booking agents at venues at which you would like to perform. You will also give copies to the local press to entice them to write a story about you or come see your show (or both). College newspapers or smaller presses might be more receptive to your demo than larger papers. But if you have a decent demo, there's no reason not to send it to everyone who writes about music in your city. Of course, you can give a demo to a record label, too. But that will happen later, after you've developed your musical talents, songwriting, and performance skills, and have a higher-quality recording to share.

Things You Can Do Today To Build Your Career
1) Start saving money to record a demo. Research local recording studio rates and their reputations.
2) Develop a budget and ask several studios what they can do for you.
3) Get into the studio as soon as you can. Local colleges of music often have recording programs and their students need to record bands. Hook up with those students and get some free studio time. Just beware that they're learning too. The finished product probably won't be professional quality.

YOUR FIRST FULL-LENGTH RECORDING

W ith the advent of digital recording equipment and the relatively low cost of manufacturing compact discs, most artists now record a full-length album before they are signed to a record label. An independently produced CD serves several important purposes. It gives you additional experience in the recording studio, it provides you with a quality full-length recording to include in your promotional package (as explained in chapter 18, "Creating Your Promotional Package"), and it provides you with a product to sell at shows and local record stores.

It is impossible to describe every tip for making a better recording in this book, and, despite what some people might say, you cannot make a $100,000 record for $4,000. However, I describe below some simple strategies that will help you make the most of your time in the studio, to make the best recording possible on a limited budget, and, hopefully, to enjoy the experience.

You should make several demo recordings, as described in chapter 15, "Recording Your First Demo," before recording your first full-length album. This process can and should be exciting and educational. It will also cost some money. Then again, no education comes free. Think of your time in the studio as a really cool college course. The good news is that a little planning and forethought can help keep your costs down.

First, before you ever go into a recording studio, even for your demo, rehearse your songs as many times as you can stand, until you are confident that you can perform them perfectly. This will limit your mistakes and save time in the studio. Chances are, you will have been performing live for quite awhile before recording and will know your songs well. Still, some rehearsal time outside your live shows can be helpful in perfecting the material.

Second, I recommend meeting with the studio engineer and/or producer (if you are using a producer) before recording your full-length album. Provide them with a demo tape or CD of all the songs you intend to record so they can get an idea of how you sound and the arrangements of your songs before you arrive at the studio. If you do not have a recording of your songs, you might invite the engineer/producer to a live performance or a rehearsal.

Discuss your goals for the recording with them, including the amount of money you have to spend. This will help them calculate how many days you can spend in the studio and how much time you will be able to spend on each song. You can also get some idea of whether or not the people at the studio believe you can accomplish your goals with the amount of money you have. These preparations will assure that everyone is on the same page when you begin to record.

Third, it saves *your* time and money if you arrive at the studio ready to work. Get adequate rest each night before recording instead of spending all night rehearsing one last time. "Cramming" didn't work the night before my calculus exam, and it won't help you to learn your songs any better, either.

Fourth, do *not* invite friends (including boyfriends, girlfriends, family members, etc.) to your recording sessions. Sure, it might be fun, but I've seen many times how the presence of extra people can be distracting and time-consuming. This will cost you money and possibly a good recording.

Fifth, believe me when I say, limit your consumption of alcohol during recording (for those of age to drink). It can slow down the whole process or become downright debilitating. I've seen some ugly fights over one band member's inability to play his or her parts properly. That's the last thing you want in the studio, where you're paying for each hour.

I know it may be tempting to pursue that rock & roll lifestyle. But remember why you're in the studio: To make the best recording possible and move closer to achieving a career in music. Alcohol will not enhance your performance. It's far better to wait until after the day's recording to celebrate.

Sixth, I learned from an experienced producer to take occasional breaks in recording and mixing, and to quit the session when you are tired. After several hours of playing and hearing the same song(s) over and over, it can become difficult to tell what really sounds good. The artists and studio professionals need energy and fresh ears to assure you get the best recording, so take a break when you need one.

Things You Can Do Today To Build Your Career
1) Rehearse your songs until they are perfect. Now you're ready to make a full-length recording.
2) Meet with several engineers and producers. Play them your material and ask for their thoughts. Discuss what you want out of the recording sessions. Work only with those people who can help you achieve your goals.
3) Don't make the recording session a big party. Remember, you're *paying* for every minute you're in the studio. Studio work is serious business. Celebrate and socialize with your friends after the recording is finished.

THE RECORDING IS DONE, BUT THE WORK'S NOT OVER

O nce you have completed the recording, you will mix the record. This is the process of mixing all the individual tracks (vocals, guitar, drums, keyboards, etc.) so that everything can be heard at the level you want. You've probably heard recordings that were not mixed well. Maybe you couldn't hear the bass drum, or maybe there was too *much* bass, or the vocals were drowned out by the guitar. A skilled engineer or producer will avoid these kinds of problems.

It is entirely acceptable for you to give your opinions during the mixing process. But by now, you should be able to trust your engineer/producer. Have the patience to listen to them and rely upon their experience to mix your recording properly.

After your record is mixed, the process moves to the next stage: Mastering. Mastering is an enhancement process that will help to improve the sound of your recording and set it apart from other recordings. You would not master your first demo, but you should master full-length recordings or demos that you send to record labels. Mastering costs can range from $50 to $500 per track, depending on the studio you use. I recommend finding a mastering facility that will master your first full-length recording for around $500 to $750. You might be able to have the record mastered at the recording studio. However, you might have to go to another facility that has mastering equipment and engineers who have experience with the equipment and the process.

After mastering is complete, the studio can provide you with both a DAT (digital audio tape) and a CD-R (recordable compact disc), which you will give to a company to manufacture and package copies of your compact discs or cassette tapes. I will not discuss all the details of the manufacturing process in this book. In fact, there are as many variables as artists: How many copies do you want? What kind of art do you want? How do you want the CD/cassette packaged? A great book about those very questions is Christian Huber's *Producing Your Own CDs: A Handbook.*

There are many competent companies that can assist you in manufacturing and packaging your recording. As with all other aspects of your career in music, do your research before committing to a deal. Ask others what companies they use, and how they like these companies. Talk to other artists, your studio, record companies in your area, or whoever might be knowledgeable. You can also ask each manufacturer for sample packages that demonstrate the quality of the company's work.

One final thing to remember: You will need to employ an artist to design the artwork for your CD or cassette, unless you're going to do it yourself. Be sure to use a designer who has experience creating art for compact discs. After the art is complete, the designer should be able to provide you with a computer disc that contains all the art for the CD/cassette and cover. The art should be properly formatted so that you can simply give this disc to the company that will manufacture and package your recording.

Things You Can Do Today To Build Your Career
1) During the mixing process, trust your engineer and/or producer. They do this for a living and won't steer you wrong. But don't be afraid to voice your opinions and preferences.
2) Don't skimp on the mastering process. It's one of those things that sets professional recordings apart from those created by amateurs.
3) Find a talented graphic artist who has experience designing CD covers and inserts. Let this person be the liaison with the CD replication plant when it comes to matters of design and packaging.

CREATING YOUR PROMOTIONAL PACKAGE

O ne tool you will need throughout your career as an artist is a promotional package, or "promo pack." I call it a résumé for recording artists. Even after you have achieved a certain level of success, you will need to send your promo pack to various music professionals and gatekeepers to demonstrate your talents and accomplishments. (I will discuss exactly who should receive your promo pack in chapter 19, "How To Use the Promotional Package.") The materials in your promo pack allow these people to assess your talent and appearance, which helps them to determine if they want to hire you, promote you, and/or enter into a contract with you.

Your promotional package will include your demo or full-length CD, a photograph, a brief biography or "bio," and favorable newspaper or magazine reviews of your latest recording or performance(s). Some promo packs may also include a video of a performance or a music video. However, unless you have a professional-quality video, I recommend not including one. Don't be overwhelmed by putting all this together. It's simply a matter of compiling the items, organizing them artistically but simply, and replacing old materials with newer, better ones as your career advances.

I talk about creating your demo tape and full-length recording in previous chapters. If you cannot afford a professional photographer, it's fine to have your photo taken by someone who has a good camera and knows how to use it. Shoot a roll or two of film in a variety of locations and select the photo that best represents the look you want. Then have high-quality copies made at your local photo store. Black-and-white photos are best, because they are easier for newspapers and other publications to print.

Some commercial companies will create a professional promotional photo for you. They will place a border around the picture, which allows you to print your name and contact information directly on the photo. (The photo should always be eight by ten inches, as anything larger will not fit in a standard envelope.) These companies will also duplicate your photos in large quantities relatively cheaply. As always, research the companies and your possibilities before having your photos duplicated. You might even know someone with a darkroom who is willing to print some photos for you. Just remember, they're not likely to be happy about making 100 copies, and if they are not skilled, your photo might not look as professional as you want.

Reviews of your shows and recordings will come over time. Starting today, collect copies of all comments about your work from anyone other than a fan. You can use reviews from print or electronic media, or even spoken comments from a public or college radio disc jockey. It's acceptable to use a compilation of comments until you obtain a full review in a local newspaper, or even better, a nationally distributed publication.

A bio is a short description of you as an artist. If you're in a group, the bio will include a short description of each member of the group (instrument played, important musical achievements, musical influences, etc.), as well as information about the group as a whole. Your bio will be a little more difficult to write early on because you do not have many experiences or successes to write about. This is not a problem. Just be creative. Write something interesting so that others will want to know more about you.

The overall quality of your promo pack will depend on factors like your current level of talent, the studio and producer you use for the recording, and your photographer. Major labels spend a lot of money for a polished package with slick printing, fancy materials, and a music video. But you can build a solid, attention-grabbing promo pack with creativity and ingenuity. And it doesn't have to be expensive. Companies like PrintingForLess.com can help you create inexpensive professionally printed promotional material. An excellent resource for more information about, and examples of, promo packs and bios is *The Billboard Guide to Publicity* by Jim Pettigrew.

After you have all the materials, draft a very brief letter to include with the package you send. The letter should look professional (print it out from a computer on decent paper) and consist of only a few sentences. This is no time to explain your dreams or accomplishments, or the reasons why you are going to be a huge success. The people reading your letter will be very busy and will appreciate your consideration in getting to the point. The letter's purpose is to get your package to the appropriate person, to identify yourself and the package contents, and to explain what you want (consideration for a record contract, a slot on an upcoming show, a review in the local newspaper, etc.). That's it. Close by thanking the reader for his or her time.

As you build your career, your promo pack will evolve along with you. Over time, you will replace older materials with new recordings, new photographs, and have new reviews in more established publications. This is no different from when I add new accomplishments to my résumé. You want to demonstrate your growing abilities, notoriety, and experience.

Things You Can Do Today To Build Your Career

1) Hire a photographer or enlist a friend who's a pretty good amateur photographer. Spend an hour or two having your picture taken in a variety of locations. Select the best one for your promo package.
2) Keep clippings of all your concert and record reviews. Photocopy the really good ones and include those in your promo package.
3) Spend some time writing your bio from the third person point of view. Even though you're just starting out and may not have that many stories to tell, try to make the bio as interesting as possible. Draw the reader in and create a desire for them to learn more about you and/or your band.

HOW TO USE THE PROMOTIONAL PACKAGE

Your promo pack will have a variety of uses throughout your career. In all cases, it is important to consider who will receive your promo pack, and to adapt it accordingly. Like a résumé, your promo pack should contain information that is most relevant to the "job" you are seeking.

When you're starting out, you will send your promo pack to clubs or other venues to obtain your first performances. You may be able to book shows at some places without a promo pack. However, it is always helpful to provide one, even at smaller venues. It's a way of setting you apart and getting attention. If possible, include printed reviews of your performances at other places.

Naturally, a club owner or booking agent will want to know what you sound like so they can determine if your style is right for the club. They also need to know if you are talented enough to perform there. The promo pack makes it a lot easier for them to decide. In addition, it demonstrates immediately that you are taking a professional approach. As someone who has owned a club and booked national bands to play there, I know this approach can really help you get a foot in the door, especially when no one knows (or cares) who you are.

You may send your promo pack to local newspapers and entertainment magazines, along with a short letter asking them to write about you and your upcoming performances. If you have a good-quality demo, you can send your promo pack to college or public radio stations and ask them to consider playing your CD. If you have them, include newspaper/ magazine clippings that review the record and/or describe other radio successes your CD has had. As your career progresses a little further, you will send your promo pack to prospective managers, attorneys, and booking agents who may be interested in working with you. Finally, your promo pack will go out to prospective record companies.

Although your friends and family might think you're the most brilliant musician on the planet, you must be objective about your level of talent when you begin to send your promo pack. The *potential* of being great is not the same as being great at that moment. Be realistic and professional. Put together the best promo pack possible, and submit the package to the right person at the right time. Always think about the person or organization receiving your promo pack. What do you want from them, and what is your likelihood of getting it?

For example, as a new artist with very little recording or performing experience, you should not mass-mail your first promo pack with a three-song demo cassette tape to major radio station music directors. You'll be wasting your money and their time, and your promo pack will be deposited directly into the trash. On the other hand, after you have recorded several demo tapes and have completed your first full-length CD, when you have been performing locally and in surrounding cities for a year, and maybe even have established relationships with weekly music magazines and have compiled a few reviews of your CD, you're in a good position to send your promo pack and CD to public and college radio stations requesting for it to be played.

The same thinking applies to newspapers and magazines. If you send your first demo to a newspaper and continually harass the writer to write a review, he or she may eventually get tired of hearing from you and review your recording. The trouble is, the review will be negative, if not downright embarrassing. You won't be including *this* review in your promo pack. And you may never get another chance to get a good interview from the music critic.

Instead of this unproductive approach, submit your promotional package simply to make industry professionals aware of you. Ask for nothing other than for the person to check out your promo package and recording. Maybe they'll review it or play it. Maybe they won't. Even if they don't, they'll know who you are, and they will appreciate your professional courtesy. This can often pay off later. As your career advances and your talent improves (as demonstrated by updated versions of your promo pack), you will have a better chance of getting some attention from these people.

The bottom line is this: You have to be patient. There are no shortcuts. You can't just make up a résumé that will qualify you to be the president of a large corporation. The necessary skills and experience for this position are gained over years. Similarly, your first promo pack won't magically make you appealing to major record labels and national radio stations. It can reflect only your skill level and successes up to this point. As your talent grows and your achievements add up over time, your promo pack will change to highlight these developments, and it will open new doors that may be closed to you right now.

Things You Can Do Today To Build Your Career
1) Make a list of everyone who should receive your promo pack. This includes booking agents and club owners, music critics at local newspapers and magazines, and perhaps local radio DJs.
2) Don't mass mail your promo pack to major labels and mainstream radio stations across the country. You won't get any response. Keep working on your career development. When the time is right, send a revised promo pack to labels and radio stations. Don't rush it. You may get only one chance to impress someone at these top markets.
3) Use your promo pack as a networking tool. After you've met someone with some influence in the industry, send him or her a promo package. This is for his or her informational use only. You aren't asking him or her to act on it in any way. You just want to start building your reputation with this person.

MUSIC CONFERENCES

Music conferences provide one of the best ways to learn about the music business and see great performances by some of the most innovative and talented artists. Some smaller conferences are one-day events with a few speakers and a performance or two by some local artists. The more established conferences last two to three days, include a trade show, and offer informative panel discussions on topics ranging from the basics ("How To Get a Record Deal") to more academic discussions ("The Future of the Music Business").

Many panels will include well-known, experienced musical artists, producers, and/or managers who provide different views on the selected topic. This can help you understand the business from the perspectives of various music professionals you may deal with over the course of your career.

At larger conferences, panel discussions usually occur during the day. In the evening, there are showcase performances of some of the best, signed and unsigned, artists in the world. These musicians rarely are in the mainstream or heard on pop radio. I always find it encouraging to be reminded that great artists can be successful without being played on pop radio stations forty times a week. It may be encouraging for you, too.

Some conferences also include a trade show, where different businesses associated with the music industry set up booths or tables. These groups may represent performance rights societies like ASCAP, BMI, or SESAC; CD manufacturers; merchandisers (such as T-shirt- and poster-manufacturing companies); music directories; music magazines; independent record labels; and/or management, public relations, or promotions companies. To make it easy for you, most conventions will hand out bags containing promotional items (also known as SWAG, or Stuff We Always Get). If you go to enough conferences, you'll build an impressive collection of lighters, free CDs, and, of course, conference programs.

Organizers of larger, more popular conferences will print a conference book listing all registrants and trade show participants. You'll find professionals from all corners of the music industry in these directories, which are excellent resources for contact information. Whether you're looking for potential band mates, labels, managers, attorneys, or anyone else in the business, this is a great place to start. Moreover, conferences give you an opportunity to speak to these people face-to-face, usually in informal settings.

Many artists use conferences to promote themselves. If it's possible, you should, too. You can create a buzz by advertising in the conference directory, placing postcards or other promotional items in the SWAG bags, and/or passing out flyers or CDs to people. These things are even more effective if you're performing at the conference. Each conference has an application for artists who wish to perform, which usually includes a form and your promotional package. (I discuss "promo packs" in the previous chapters.) Even if you never get chosen to perform, attending a music conference is a great way to learn about the music business, hear great music, see experienced artists perform, make important contacts, and learn different ways to develop as an artist.

Billboard magazine sponsors many music conferences. Some of the more established music conferences are South by Southwest in Austin, Texas; North by Northwest in Seattle; the CMJ Music Marathon in New York City; and the Winter Music Conference in Miami. Many smaller but credible conferences are held all over the country. You can find more information by searching for "music conferences" on the Internet.

In addition, several music-industry directories list music conferences all over the world, along with contact information. *Recording Industry Sourcebook*, *Musician's Atlas*, or *Billboard Musician's Guide to Touring and Promotion* are three such directories. Each has a Web site that explains how to obtain a copy of the directories.

Don't rule out attending a local music conference or seminar in your own city. By supporting the smaller conferences, you help them grow into more established events. Check your local music-industry publications or businesses to find listings in your city. Here again, an Internet search can be helpful.

Things You Can Do Today To Build Your Career
1) Find a local music conference or seminar and attend. Go to the workshops and attend as many of the live shows as you can. Critique the performances and compare the level of musicianship to your own band.
2) Save your money and attend one of the large, established music conferences, such as South by Southwest in Austin, Texas, or CMJ Music Marathon in New York City.
3) Consider promoting your band at a music conference via printed materials or a live showcase.

PART
THREE

PROFESSIONAL
PERSONNEL

SOME PROFESSIONALS YOU WILL NEED

21

*I*t is impossible to have a successful career as an artist in the music indus- try without assistance. This multibillion-dollar business is complicated and sophisticated. It's difficult for an artist to focus on his or her cre- ative development and keep up with all the business aspects, as well. Yes, to protect yourself, you do need to learn as much as possible about the busi- ness. But you will also have to rely upon professionals to help your career, both during the development stage and after you become successful.

I describe some of the roles and responsibilities of these professionals in detail throughout this chapter. Eventually, you will need (at least) a profes- sional manager, an entertainment attorney, a booking agent, a business manager, and a publicist. As in any business, you need to research the peo- ple with whom you plan to sign contracts, or entrust your career decisions and money.

You can do this research in two ways. First, ask people in your local music scene about reputable music professionals (managers, attorneys, etc.) in your area. Second, meet with these professionals. Ask them about their experience and whom they represent, or have represented. If possible, check with the artists these professionals have represented to find out if they did a good job.

A professional manager provides advice regarding career development. He or she will be your main liaison to the music industry, including record labels, concert promoters, publishing companies, attorneys, booking agents, publicists, etc. By dealing with these third parties, the professional manager frees up your time to write songs, record, tour, and make promotional appearances.

You will also need an entertainment attorney from time to time to discuss your legal needs. For instance, you will want an experienced attorney to negotiate or draft major contracts you are going to sign (e.g., management, recording, publishing, or endorsement contracts).

In addition, you will need a separate professional, other than the manager, to seek out employment for you as an artist. This is why they invented booking agents. Your booking agent will have relationships with venue owners, promoters, or festival organizers. He or she will send out promotional packages and communicate with these various contacts to obtain employment for you or your band.

A business manager will handle your music-related income and expenses, to make sure all your accounting is in order, your bills and taxes are paid, etc. A business manager is usually an accountant or CPA (certified public accountant). Until you make enough money to pay for a business manager, your professional manager may assume this role.

Your publicist is responsible for promoting your musical career by getting exposure for you—through stories, interviews, or music reviews—in newspapers, television, radio, the Internet, etc. If you can't afford a publicist, do this stuff yourself. If you have a manager, he or she can help.

All of these professionals decide to work with an artist before or during that artist's initial development because they believe the artist has some talent that would be worth representing. In other words, it's a business decision, which means you have to make a good impression on them, too. You may have a lot of talent, but you also need to approach them in a professional manner, with some knowledge of the business and an understanding of what each side can expect from a potential relationship.

In fact, these professionals are also a type of gatekeeper to the industry, and you should have developed to a certain point before you contact them. You won't send your first two-song demo to Warner Bros., but you might send it to a local producer, manager, or entertainment attorney. This person can then evaluate your talent and level of development to determine if he or she (1) wants to work with you, and (2) can assist your career advancement.

Things You Can Do Today To Build Your Career

1) Realize that you will need the help of others in order to make it in this business. You couldn't possibly learn everything there is to know about every aspect of the business. That's why you'll eventually need to team with an entertainment attorney, manager, booking agent, publicist, etc.

2) When meeting other successful local musicians, always ask them about their experiences with managers, attorneys, publicists, etc. You'll soon see a pattern among professionals to seek out and those to avoid.

WHAT DOES AN ENTERTAINMENT ATTORNEY DO?

An entertainment attorney's primary job is to advise and counsel clients (i.e., you) about legal aspects of the entertainment industry. Common responsibilities of your attorney will be to draft and negotiate contracts for you with third parties, such as record and publishing companies, managers, booking agents, and producers. Your attorney will also prepare your copyright or trademark registrations, and advise you on issues as diverse as goal setting, things to consider when choosing a manager or record company, and your career direction.

We have all heard horror stories about artists signing bad deals. I've seen the aftermath, and it's not pretty. The single most important job of your entertainment attorney is to help you to avoid these kinds of disasters. The attorney will advise you and protect your interests before you sign any agreements with other industry professionals or, ultimately, record companies. He or she will make sure you understand the contract, and that the contract is up to industry standards. In other words, your attorney's main objective is to do everything he or she can to make sure you enter into a fair agreement with a reputable record label, producer, manager, etc.

So before you sign any contract in the entertainment industry, always get the advice of an entertainment attorney. Simply having an attorney does not guarantee you'll get the best contract (as in any other profession, some attorneys are better than others). However, it greatly increases the likelihood that you'll understand the contract you are signing, and that you won't get burned.

One thing all entertainment attorneys do *not* do—despite the popular myth—is seek out and secure record deals for artists: A process known as "shopping" an artist to record labels. It is true that some entertainment attorneys perform this service, but very few succeed in getting their clients signed to a deal. The ones who do succeed almost always are working with artists who already have spent years developing themselves and have had some success. A reputable, experienced entertainment attorney will explain this to you.

Many artists and/or their parents want to be told that if they spend a ton of money on a demo tape and hire an expensive lawyer, they'll get a deal from a major label. You can try this, but I strongly recommend that you don't. You'll probably end up with a great-sounding demo, no record deal, and a lot less money.

If you find an attorney who says he or she will shop your material to labels, be cautious. Before writing a big check, or even entering into an agreement with the attorney to send your material around, ask a lot of questions regarding his or her experience in the entertainment industry, who he or she has represented, and how many successes he or she has had getting record contracts for artists. The fact is you can't buy your way into the music industry. You get there through development and hard work. That's what this book is all about.

Unfortunately, record companies perpetuate the myth, telling artists that entertainment attorneys can shop their materials. They tell artists this only because their label does not accept material directly from artists and instead wants materials submitted by someone with whom the label has a relationship. This process is best left to successful managers or producers who have a relationship with the label(s) you wish to contact *and* experience shopping artists.

Things You Can Do Today To Build Your Career
1) Learn about what entertainment attorneys actually do. Do not spend a lot of money hiring an attorney to shop your material.
2) Talk with other local artists and find out if they've been burned by a legal agreement in the past. What can you learn from those mistakes?
3) Read about some well-known legal battles in Stan Soocher's book, *They Fought the Law: Rock Music Goes to Court.*

WHEN DO YOU NEED AN ENTERTAINMENT ATTORNEY?

An entertainment attorney should be your first professional contact in the music industry. A good attorney can help guide you through each step of your career, help you make decisions about how to achieve your goals, and assist you in approaching industry "gatekeepers." For these reasons, I recommend finding an entertainment attorney early in your career, someone to advise you along the way.

Most entertainment attorneys will charge a nominal fee to counsel you on career development matters. During these consultations, you can get answers to many of your questions, insight into the industry, and valuable help in advancing your career in music.

It is really beneficial to have this kind of direction, and to have someone looking out for your best interest—even if you have to pay for it—from the very start of your career. You won't have to sign an exclusive contract to consult with an entertainment attorney, who will be available whenever you want to set an appointment. Once you find a manager, it will become his or her job to advise you about career issues, while your attorney will continue to counsel you in legal matters.

Exactly when you first contact an entertainment attorney is, of course, up to you. I really don't like to set absolute rules, or say "never" or "always," because every situation is different. But once you start dealing with contracts, the absolutes apply. Never sign *anything* related to your music career, except an autograph, without the counsel of an entertainment attorney. This is not an option, but a requirement. Protect yourself.

No matter what your music-related goals may be, this is a business based on contractual agreements. Before signing one, always have it reviewed by an attorney. This will help you to know exactly what you are signing, what you are committing to, and what you will receive in return. And always seek the advice of an experienced attorney who is knowledgeable about the music industry. In other words, your Aunt Sara's neighbor, Bob, who practices real-estate law, is not the guy you need representing you on a record deal.

Some artists believe that employing an entertainment attorney will hurt their chances of securing the deal because the attorney will intimidate the other side or somehow ruin the deal. This is an unfortunate misconception. As described in the previous chapter, your entertainment attorney will advise you and help to protect you from signing a bad deal. It is simply the attorney's job to negotiate a better deal with the record company or other industry professionals.

Reputable companies, managers, and other music-industry professionals know this and will actually welcome your use of an attorney. No major record or publishing company will negotiate a contract with an artist who is not represented by an entertainment attorney. And no reputable professional will object to your having an attorney review an agreement before you sign. If the person or company with whom you are talking does not want you to hire an attorney, or says you do not need an attorney, or breaks off negotiations because you sought out counsel, then you absolutely should not be in a contract with that person or company anyway.

You may prefer to save money and go without an entertainment attorney. It always is your choice. But know this: During my years of experience, I have spent a lot more time (and made a lot more money) trying to get artists out of bad deals than negotiating moderate to good deals for clients who hired me at the start. As the old saying goes, "You can pay me now or pay me later." Bottom line: Your attorney's fees are as much a cost of doing business in the music industry as your guitar or studio time.

Things You Can Do Today To Build Your Career
1) Accept the idea that an attorney will be necessary. Start asking around for some referrals.
2) Consult with an entertainment attorney regarding all contract or legal matters before taking any action.
3) Before signing anything, consult with an attorney.

Finding an Entertainment Attorney

*I*t will take a little effort to find the right entertainment attorney. At the start, you should look for an attorney with three qualities: A good reputation with others in the entertainment industry, knowledge of the music business, and experience with copyright law.

Some state or local bar associations (the organizations that regulate attorneys) can help identify attorneys in your area who practice entertainment law. Music industry directories, such as *Recording Industry Sourcebook* and *Musician's Atlas*, are other great resources to help you find the right attorney. And don't forget about the Internet. These options are better than just looking in the yellow pages, because they are designed to point out entertainment attorneys (and not just give you a list of attorneys in all fields). No matter where you search, be sure to research the criteria noted above to give yourself the best chance of finding a good entertainment attorney.

The best, most reliable references will be your trusted colleagues in the local or national music community. Depending on your legal needs, an attorney in another state may be quite capable of representing you in the music business, via telephone and fax or e-mail, if necessary. You will need to discuss this with the attorney. Finally, before placing your career in an attorney's hands, schedule a meeting (either in person or on the telephone) to discuss his or her knowledge, type and years of experience, current and previous clients, etc.

Most attorneys will charge a fee to talk to them. Like everyone else, they're in business to make money and their time is valuable to their clients. If they're talking to you, they cannot be talking to their clients (i.e., making money). I usually charge a nominal hourly fee of $50 to meet with an artist. This allows me to provide consultation without the artist having to take out a loan to pay for legal fees. It's a great way for an artist to have my full attention for a reasonable cost. Many, if not most, entertainment attorneys operate the same way. The fee charged for services will depend on the attorney's experience, reputation, and location.

Remember to call ahead and schedule an appointment, and understand that you probably won't be able to speak to the attorney when you first call. When you call, confirm with the staff that the attorney sees clients for consultation on entertainment matters, explain your situation, and ask what the cost for one hour of the attorney's time is for this type of matter. You could inquire if the attorney charges a different rate for general consultations, vs. specific matters such as negotiating or drafting contracts. You might even ask the staff if they can provide you with some information about the attorney's experience. The firm may well have a Web site that answers some of these questions, so you should do an Internet search prior to calling.

Prepare before your consultation with the attorney. This will save the attorney's time and your money. Write down the questions you want to ask and the items you want to discuss with the attorney so you cover all the bases. I often ask the client to write down the questions and give me a copy in advance, so I can get an idea about what the client is expecting to discuss during our hour consultation.

If you haven't been able to find information about the attorney's experience, don't be embarrassed to ask. I welcome prospective clients to ask me this question. It means they are doing their homework, and that they're probably responsible and serious. I respect that. Other attorneys should, also.

Ask the attorney if he or she can counsel you on the development of your career, what his or her rates are, and for what, exactly he or she charges. Some attorneys may charge a lower rate for consultations than for contract negotiations. Ask the attorney to describe how he or she can help your career.

If you are satisfied and comfortable with the responses, you can begin asking substantive questions. Ask the attorney to describe the best way for you to proceed in your career, and to identify the kinds of issues for which you should seek his or her assistance. Hopefully, by the end of the meeting, you will have found an entertainment attorney to assist you in your legal and career matters. But if not, don't feel bad. This is an important professional decision, and you need to get it right. If you're not comfortable with this attorney, continue your search until you find one who is right for you.

Things You Can Do Today To Build Your Career
1) When looking for an entertainment lawyer, get a referral from friends, colleagues, persons in the industry, or from your state or local bar association.
2) Consult the *Recording Industry Sourcebook* or *Musician's Atlas* for more entertainment attorney listings.
3) Schedule a consultation appointment with an entertainment attorney before committing to a long-term relationship. It will cost you a few bucks, but it will give you a chance to learn more about the lawyer and explain your specific needs.

What Does a Manager Do?

O ne of your most important choices as a musical artist will be selecting your professional manager. This individual will represent you to other people, provide music-business counseling, and guide your career. He or she will probably be your closest friend in the music business, your most trusted professional partner. Therefore, it is critical that you consider your choice of manager very carefully. The manager's exact duties will usually depend on the artist's level of success. I will focus below on the things a manager would do for a developing artist, like you.

Artist management is the business of enhancing or furthering an artist's career. Your manager will provide many important services for you. First, he or she will create opportunities for you to get new experiences that you otherwise would get only through frustrating years of trial and error. This will be especially important early in your career. In addition, your manager will devise and carry out a plan to promote you to the public. And after your career has advanced to a certain point, he or she will work with your label, booking agent, publicist, etc. This will leave you free to write, perform, and generally do what you do best: Be an artist.

Right from the start, you will benefit from your manager's knowledge of the best ways to promote and develop you in the immediate community—whether through clubs, college or public radio stations, record stores, print media, or most likely, a combination of those. Your manager will probably have spent years building knowledge, resources, and relationships. You will get the benefit of those experiences without having to go through them yourself. In this way, a manager can help to speed up your development and allow you to focus on constructive, creative things, like improving your musical and performance skills and writing better songs.

No, the manager is not there to put up flyers advertising your show while you sleep off a hangover. Until you can afford to hire a work force, *you* are the work force. However, depending on your relationship, your manager might design your flyer, take it to get printed, and help you place it on windshields of cars at clubs around town.

Your manager knows you will eventually need a strong promotional package to send out to independent labels. He or she will help you create a package that represents your artistic talents most effectively. The manager also knows that labels are looking for artists with (1) good songs, (2) an ability to record, and (3) a solid live performance. Your short-term goal is to meet these three criteria. Your manager will help you create and implement a plan to develop your talents so you can accomplish this goal.

Your manager will also handle a lot of administrative things that can generally make you crazy. For example, he or she will (1) arrange for you to go into the recording studio as often as possible; (2) encourage you to practice and give you feedback to improve your live performance; (3) book your shows, or hire a booking agent to find you gigs to help you improve your performance and build a fan base; (4) arrange to have your photographs made for publicity and promotions; and (5) encourage the media to review your performances and/or recordings (these reviews will be included in your promotional package).

It is important to mention that California and New York have specific restrictions regarding a manager obtaining employment for an artist (i.e., booking shows), unless the manager also has a talent agent's license. I recommend that you research this issue in your state to determine the limits (if any) on your manager's ability to act as your booking agent. And, obviously, you will want to consult with an entertainment attorney before signing a management contract.

Things You Can Do Today To Build Your Career
1) Remember that hiring a manager doesn't mean you now have a personal assistant. But you will have someone knowledgeable in your corner to assist in your career development.
2) Once you've hired a manager, be open to his or her ideas. But be sure to define your goals clearly so he or she can help you attain them in the easiest, most professional way.
3) Ask your manager to help you with some of the administrative tasks with which artists are saddled: Creating and compiling a promotional package, creating and printing concert flyers, etc.

When Do You Need a Manager?

A paradox presents itself early in an artist's career. While you will certainly need advice throughout your career, you probably will need the most guidance when you are first getting started. Unfortunately, until you've gained a small amount of success, you won't be able to attract an experienced manager. So what are you supposed to do?

If you understand the purpose of a manager, you will be able to advance your career on your own, until you find a manager. As explained in the previous chapter, your manager's most important jobs are to (1) devise and carry out a plan to promote you (the artist) to the public and help you build a fan base, and (2) work with your label, booking agent, publicist, etc., so you can concentrate on writing songs and developing your musical and performance skills.

There is a common misconception that a manager will develop an artist's raw talent. This isn't true. We've invented vocal and performance coaches and music teachers to develop musical and performance skills. The manager's job is to help an artist who is already developing him or herself to leap forward in his or her career. The good news is you don't need a manager to improve your skills, gain valuable experience, and begin to enjoy success in the music industry. You can simply begin by doing the things set forth in this book.

Many artists start their careers with representation from friends or family members. While there is usually a certain level of trust built into this kind of arrangement, your friends and family probably don't have enough knowledge about the business to help you develop your career very far. Nonetheless, they can probably help in some ways, even if it's just doing some legwork or providing moral support. In the beginning, that may be good enough.

But as your career progresses, you will present your music and image to record labels and other third parties. The quality of your presentation is vitally important to your success as a musician/performer. Labels want to know that your representative is knowledgeable about the business and can continue to improve your career. When you get to the point of talking to labels, if not before, you'll probably need a professional manager.

When an artist starts making money, his or her manager is paid a percentage of that income. When you start out, you will be more concerned with development and opportunities than with making money. This is proper, but it means that at first, you will not be able to pay a manager. (This is part of the reason most professional managers will wait until you achieve a certain level of success before they will work with you.) That's okay. I have met, known, and represented many successful artists who did not have managers, even when they signed their first record deals. So don't worry if you don't have a manager in your first year (or five). You'll be in good company.

Unfortunately, no bell will ring when you have reached the right point in your career to obtain a professional manager. Many times, this decision is based upon knowing what specific managers are looking for. For example, many managers of young pop artists want to begin working with those artists very early, so they can help to refine that talent. Other managers prefer to work with artists who already have developed their skills and careers to a higher level.

Although it can be difficult to know exactly when to seek out a manager, there are some rough guidelines to help you. If you have taken the following steps in your career, you are in a position to approach a manager who has had some success in managing other artists in your location.

- Develop a repertoire of enough quality songs to perform a thirty- to forty-five-minute set.
- Perform those songs live with some success locally.
- Record at least three of those songs on a quality recording.
- Put together a promotional package showing your talents.

Of course, there is no law that says you need a manager at this point. You may continue to develop yourself, and even get a deal with a reputable independent label. If you make it that far on your own, you'll be able to approach even more successful managers, because you will have demonstrated that you have drive, talent, ambition, and an ability to make money in this business. Having persevered through the difficult early times, you are beginning to establish yourself. You won't have to convince people; they will be able to see the results of your work. This puts you in a good position to shop around for different managers.

Until that time, though, concentrate on creative development and being the best performer you can be. Assuming you have talent, your early hard work will create later opportunities for finding a manager (and other industry professionals) to take you to another level.

Things You Can Do Today To Build Your Career
1) Keep concentrating on your creative development. Remember, even once you have a manager, it's still up to you to tend to your musical and performance skills. Most managers will not help develop your artistry. That's not their role.
2) While you may have a friend or family member manage you now, you'll need to move on and hire a professional as your career progresses. Record labels and venues expect a very professional presentation, and you'll need a manager to break through some barriers for you. An unskilled friend or your mom just won't be able to do that.
3) After developing a thirty-minute live performance, performing locally with some success, recording three songs, and compiling a promotional package, you can then begin shopping your package to a manager.

FINDING A MANAGER

T his chapter is really more about the qualities to seek in a manager than about actually finding the manager. Unfortunately, there's no hotline you can call or place you can go to order a manager: "One professional manager please, and could I get a gold record with that?" I will provide some general advice to help you locate a manager. But first, I'll discuss the qualities to look for in this person to whom you will entrust at least part of your career in the music industry.

Some managers work with new, developing artists who have achieved some success locally. These individuals can be instrumental to your career, and it is appropriate for them to be paid and given enough time to enhance your career. I refer to these managers—who work with developing artists or artists on independent labels—as middle-level managers. While there is a growing need for these types of managers, it is hard for them to sustain a living representing only local or developing bands that do not make a lot of money. A manager who takes 15% of the $50 you earned from your one show this month will have a difficult time paying the telephone bill.

For this reason, a manager usually can afford to work with only one or two developing bands at a time, along with several bands that make money. And yes, I said several bands. Unless you're making enough money to pay your manager's full salary, he or she will need to represent other artists. As they say, "It's not personal. Just business." In fact, this arrangement can work in your favor. The experiences and connections your manager gains while working with other artists may benefit you later.

One way to find a middle-level manager is to network and ask around within your local music community. There are also several good resource books and directories that list names of managers, and sometimes their clients. A few such resources are *Billboard* magazine's *International Guide to Talent & Touring, Musician's Atlas,* and *Recording Industry Sourcebook.* The Internet is a good place to start your search for these types of references and directories.

After you have identified a few potential candidates, based on their location and any other information you can gather, send your promotional package to these managers as you would anyone else in this business. Include a short cover letter that tells a little about yourself, says where you're located, and explains that you're looking for a manager who works with developing artists. Expect little or no response. Many managers do not work with developing talent, and most are very busy managing their own artists. Your search for a manager will not be easy, and you may feel discouraged at times. But remember, it's not personal…just business. With a realistic approach and persistence, you *will* find the right manager.

The best way to determine if a manager can help you is to decide upon your immediate and long-term goals, and to have a realistic perspective about your present level of success. Before hiring a manager, ask what he or she thinks of your goals and what he or she will do to help you achieve them. This is, after all, the manager's job. Your manager should be fully supportive of your goals as an artist and should help you achieve them, or be able to provide solid reasons why the goals you've set should be revised. Discussing these goals with the manager is also a good way to learn about his or her qualifications and knowledge of the music business. It should definitely help you decide if you want to enter into an agreement with this person.

There is no single right way to manage an artist's career. However, there *is* a way to determine a manager's effectiveness: Results. Obviously, you want a manager who will bring results and help you meet your goals. When you begin speaking to potential managers, treat the process professionally. In fact, managers are interviewing for a job with your music "business." Then again, you are also being interviewed, especially if you have not achieved a lot of success yet.

While your talks do not have to occur in a formal setting (sometimes, the club you're playing later that night can be the best place), you should be organized and have some questions prepared in advance. You want to obtain as much information as possible about the manager's experience, ideas, qualifications, and traits.

What should you look for? The manager should appear to be responsible and well organized. He or she should be a good planner and adviser, should have an ability to strategize, and appear to have good general-business skills. These traits can help make up for any lack of experience he or she may have in the music business.

To find out if prospective managers have these qualities, ask who they have represented, how long they have been managing artists, how they approach managing (i.e., what is their management style?), what other qualifications they have that make them good managers, and what they would do to help your career. Two of my favorite questions are, "What will be your long-term plan for me if we sign a management agreement?" and "If we sign a management agreement today, what are you going to do for me tomorrow?"

Before deciding on a manager, you should have several meetings to discuss your goals and each manager's ideas for managing you. At the same time, you should be consulting with an entertainment attorney. The attorney can give you additional advice on questions to ask and what to look for during your manager "interview" process.

Once you have decided on your manager, he or she will offer you a management agreement or you will ask for a contract. *Do not* sign this (or any other) agreement before taking it to an entertainment attorney for review and discussion. I understand you know how to read. But these agreements will be written in a different style, and almost a different language, from what most people are accustomed to. Chances are very good that you will not understand the ramifications of the agreement without an attorney's assistance. To put it bluntly, you may well end up hurting yourself if you sign something without first having it reviewed by an entertainment attorney. I know that may sound self-serving, but I assure you, it's not. In fact, this warning is just part of my job in this book: To help protect you.

At the very minimum, have an attorney briefly review the contract, explain the major terms of the agreement, and confirm whether or not it is within industry standards. Protect yourself. Regardless of what you may have heard, if you sign a three-year contract with a manager, you will not be able to simply fire him or her without some legal consequences.

I suggest that you hire an attorney to review and revise the management agreement. The goal is not to negotiate a contract that gives you every benefit, but to assure that the agreement is balanced. Your attorney will then present the revised contract to the prospective manager and negotiate terms, rationally and professionally, possibly suggesting additional compromises from both parties that will result in a fair deal for everyone.

Most entertainment attorneys approach this process in a creative, not adversarial, manner. It is our job to negotiate a deal that satisfies both sides, and to advise our client (you) so the client can make an educated decision when presented with his or her choices. As I said before, you can pay me a little now or pay me a lot later. It's better to spend the money up front and get a fair contract, than to spend a lot more a year from now to get out of a bad deal.

Things You Can Do Today To Build Your Career
1) Talk with some bands whose reputations you admire. Ask who their manager is and try to set up an appointment to see if his or her services would work for your band as well.
2) Consult some of the music-industry directories (such as *Musician's Atlas* or the *Recording Industry Sourcebook*) and find a few managers in your area. Give them a call and see if you can set up an appointment to discuss your career.
3) Once you find a manager you'd like to work with, draw up your goals and make sure he or she can help you attain them. Then, consult an entertainment attorney before signing any agreement. *MusicBusinessMadeSimple.com* archives downloadable management agreements for you reference.

THE BOOKING AGENT

Your manager's job entails a wide variety of tasks that help advance your career. But your booking agent, or talent agent, has only one function: To obtain employment for you. A booking agent's job is to schedule, or "book," your live performances in different venues, such as clubs, theaters, festivals, arenas, etc. Your level of success as an artist will determine the level of interest booking agents have in working with you.

As with professional management, there are different levels of booking agents, from those who book local clubs to those at international talent agencies like Creative Artists Agency or the William Morris Agency. Your level of success and the level of your agent can have a big impact on how often you perform or tour, and how much money you make.

Several national music-business resource books and directories list regional and national booking agents. Many music organizations also compile directories for local music businesses. Some of these resources are your local or state music-industry directory (which you can find on the Internet), *Billboard* magazine's *International Guide to Talent & Touring*, and *Recording Industry Sourcebook*. However, most of these resources list national booking agents. When you're starting out, you need someone local.

It can be difficult for a new artist to find a manager; it might not be easy to find a booking agent early in your career, either. You haven't achieved much success yet, and your first booking agent probably won't make much money from your performances. Start your search with local or regional booking agents who have experience booking other groups that are at about your level of success. You can probably get some good leads by networking and asking other bands/artists for names and references of booking agents who work with artists in your area.

In addition, you want someone who represents artists whose music is similar to yours. This way, the agent will know where to book you and will have relationships with clubs whose patrons are familiar with your genre of music. Very possibly, the agent will even be able to book you in other towns/cities in your area, thereby exposing new markets to your music. The booking agent will also be able to book you on shows with other artists he or she represents. This is a very helpful and important part of the process of obtaining new fans.

Like a manager, a booking agent cannot take on too many developing groups because he or she receives a percentage of the amount you are paid for a show (typically 10% plus expenses). If you're not making much (or anything) from your shows, a booking agent may decide not to work with you until you're a little more established. You may ask, "Why don't I just get my manager to book me and save the 10%?" Because it is not your manager's job to book you. In fact, some states, like California and New York, restrict the ability of a manager to book your shows.

Because it will be difficult for you to attract a booking agent early on, and your manager (if you have one) probably won't be booking your shows, you will almost certainly have to start out by booking your own shows. Almost every band and artist I have known has done this at some point in their careers. It's part of the development process, even for an artist who is enjoying a small amount of success. Until you can afford to pay a professional, you will be your own booking agent.

And until you build a relationship with local venues and develop a fan base, you will play for little or no money. That's the way it works. If you don't bring in enough people to make money for the venue, you shouldn't expect the venue to pay you. Everyone goes through this. Early on, focus on opportunities to perform. Get in front of people, develop your performance skills, and build your fan base. Even though you may not be getting paid, you are definitely benefiting from these experiences, and it's far better to play for free than not perform at all.

Over time, more people will become familiar with you and attend your performances. Then, venues will begin to pay you. And you will be able to consider hiring a booking agent to get you more shows... to play in front of more people and make more money. And so on.

Sometimes, your initial opportunity to play at a venue will be opening for another, more established band or artist who knows you and gets you on the bill. Once you get your chance, make sure you give them a good show (and try to bring in a good crowd). Even if the room is almost empty, you may be playing for the venue owner, a concert promoter, or the person who books talent to play at the venue. So give them your best performance and demonstrate a good attitude. This will make things a lot easier when you or your future booking agent contacts the venue to inquire about another opportunity to play there.

Things You Can Do Today To Build Your Career
1) Start by walking a mile in a booking agent's shoes: Be your own booking agent. Get experience booking shows at a variety of local venues. This will give you a solid idea of why you'll need a professional booking agent as your career progresses and what he or she actually does. A live performance or booking agent agreement can be downloaded at *MusicBusinessMadeSimple.com.*
2) Ask the owners of the clubs you play if they can recommend a booking agent. They'll tell you who successfully books artists in your local area—and beyond.
3) Book as many gigs as you can. Build your fan base and perfect your live performance. After that, you are ready to send your promotional package to local and regional booking agents.

WHAT DOES A PRODUCER DO?

*B*y definition, a producer is the person who oversees production of the artist's recording(s). Producers will participate in the recording/mixing/mastering process, more or less, depending on their level of experience and skill, and on the skills of the other professionals involved. Some producers have the technical expertise actually to be the sound engineer, which means they operate the equipment that records the songs as the artist performs in the studio. Some producers with musical ability may play a musical instrument on the recording and/or help the artist to write and arrange songs.

But the producer's most important function is to coordinate the recording process. He or she directs the artist, musicians, and recording technicians, while attempting to get the sound and song arrangements that the artist, producer, and record label want.

A successful producer once told me it's not his job to change the artist, but to help the artist do what he does, and to do it right in three-and-a-half minutes. With that in mind, a good producer will have several traits. First, a producer with musical and technical skills can really help the production run smoothly. He or she will understand the process that both the artist and the engineer are going through and will be able to explain or demonstrate how to achieve the desired results. In fact, most great producers are also musicians, and have been, or have performed with, recording artists.

Another critical trait to look for in a producer is the ability to communicate and stay cool under pressure. Stress can run high in studio sessions. There are long days and nights, disagreements, and pressure to perform and get the right sound. Egos often clash with fatigue. Occasionally, sparks and beer bottles begin to fly. A producer must work through these problems and keep everyone calm and focused. Sometimes, this is the most difficult job of all.

Of course, a producer also needs to understand the business and the costs of recording. Whether the artist or the record label is paying for studio time, it is the producer's responsibility to make sure the recording project is completed within the budget allotted.

Some producers just don't care about budget. I know one who allowed a band to spend more than $500,000 recording an album that bombed, even after the band's previous album—recorded for less than $100,000—was successful. He'd show up late for recording sessions and allow the band to play video games while the clock was ticking. He knew that any part of the $500,000 not spent on recording would have gone into the band's pocket, but he clearly wasn't looking out for the band's best interest. I'm not suggesting that he should have cut corners in the recording process, but what this producer did is irresponsible and unprofessional.

I talk a lot about how you (the artist) must be professional in all aspects of your musical career. Similarly, it is absolutely appropriate for you to demand professionalism from the so-called "professionals" you work with, including producers. They are working for you; make sure they work in your best interest.

An experienced and talented producer can be critical to an artist's success by providing guidance, a well-produced record, and an innovative and new sound. The producer can also play a key role in writing the music and the songs to be recorded by the artist.

Recently, a new kind of producer has arisen in the rap, pop, and hip-hop musical genres. I refer to this type of professional as a "producer of tracks." He or she wears two hats: One as the creator of the music and one as the producer of the recording of that music. The "producer of tracks" creates and records the music. After that, the artist records vocals to go with the music. Some "producers of tracks" will help the artist to complete production of the vocals, but most will not. Instead, the artist will employ a different producer to mix the vocals with the music to obtain a final version of the song.

In any case, the producer must make sure that whatever you record captures your true sound and makes you sound as good as possible, no matter how far your career has advanced. I once represented a band that had great songs and had a huge following, based on their live performances.

Unfortunately, on their first independent record deal, the label insisted that they use an inexperienced producer who was a friend of the label's owner. Predictably, the band was not very happy with the results.

After the recording was completed and mastered, the band's singer and main writer told me that, in his view, "those songs were lost forever." It's sad that those great songs will now always leave a bad impression on the band, their fans, music critics, and radio stations. A producer can really make that much difference.

Things You Can Do Today To Build Your Career
1) Get a referral from local artists or music-industry professionals for producers in your area.
2) Listen to popular records that match your musical genre. What stylistic elements are the same? Did the same engineer or producer work on several of these albums? Can you get a feel for the "sound" of each engineer and producer?
3) Visit *Grammy.com*, the National Academy of Recording Arts & Sciences (NARAS) Web site. Do a search for Grammy winners in the "Producer of the Year" category. Go to the library and listen to those albums. What similarities do they share? Tell your producer what records you like the *sound* of.

When Do You Need a Producer?

As a musical artist, you will almost certainly use a producer at some point when you go to a studio to record your songs. If you are thinking about hiring a studio producer, the two main factors to consider are how much the producer can help you and how much his or her services will cost. This decision will be based, in large part, on the purpose of the recording. It's probably not worth the money to hire a producer for your very first demos. However, you probably will want the guidance of a producer when it comes time to record your full-length recordings.

If you are not using musicians in the studio for your musical tracks, then you will employ a "producer of tracks" to create and record music for you. I explain the role of a "producer of tracks" in the previous chapter. After this music is created and recorded, you will need to hire a producer to work with you in the studio to record and mix your vocals with the music created by the "producer of tracks."

If you are about to record your first demo in a small, simple recording studio (maybe even in someone's home), there is no reason to pay a producer. The recording engineer may help you a little in the recording process, even though his or her primary function is simply to record your songs. Sure, this won't sound like a major-label release, but its purpose is to gain experience—and maybe a little exposure—not to impress the people at Warner Bros.

At this early point in your career, it's most productive to focus on developing your musical skills and live performance, and on recording as often and as much as possible to develop your recording skills. Of course, studio time costs money, and a producer's fee just adds to the bill. At first, you probably won't be able to afford this luxury. Don't worry. As I explain in detail in chapter 15, "Recording Your First Demo," your first recordings don't have to be very expensive. And they don't require a producer. Just do the best you can to get a decent recording and keep moving forward.

However, it's not unreasonable for developing artists to seek some additional guidance in the studio. If you want to hire a producer, work out an hourly rate or flat fee for the producer's services and pay as you go. (Make a similar arrangement with the studio, and just pay them for the time you use.) Some developing artists with limited funds compromise by hiring a producer for one or two tracks (maybe the two strongest songs) and self-produce the rest of the record with the aid of the engineer. This can be a good option for you, too.

There is no question that a talented producer can make you sound better. He or she will help you while recording your songs, and will work with the engineer to obtain the best sound, based on his or her knowledge of the recording equipment and your level of development as an artist. You just have to weigh the benefits and costs and decide what is best for you. Ultimately, you won't really *need* a producer until you are getting ready to make a recording for prospective managers, booking agents, or record labels, or until you're preparing to record your first full-length recording.

But the decision about when to use a producer is always yours. Being objective about your level of development and remembering the purpose of your recording will help you to decide. If you want to use a producer at any stage, try to find one who is experienced and known for working with developing artists who are at about the same stage in their careers as you. I also recommend using local producers at first. Some may have their own studios and will engineer, as well as produce, your recording. So you get two professionals for the price of one.

Some people, especially in the country and pop music markets, believe that an artist with raw talent and little development should immediately go out and hire a big-name producer, book time in a famous (and, no doubt, expensive) recording studio, and hire top-notch studio musicians, all to record songs that were written by professional songwriters. Beware. This philosophy is popular among producers and/or managers who spot raw talent and want to try to obtain a record deal without taking the time to develop an artist properly.

Naturally, the producer who persuades an artist to take this approach will get paid, along with the studio, musicians, etc. Guess who will be paying all those bills. That's right: You, the artist. You can assume this will be expensive. You can also assume the producer will get his or her fee, even if you don't obtain a record deal. Beware of anyone who offers instant fame and wealth. As the old saying goes, "If it sounds too good to be true, it probably is."

You should also be cautious if a producer attempts to persuade you to enter into a long-term written contract stating that he or she will provide free services in exchange for an interest in your songs and recordings. I advocate these types of deals only in special situations, and *never* without prior consultation with an entertainment attorney. After you have recorded several demos, you may well receive interest from an experienced and successful producer. Fantastic! However, you will still want to consult an entertainment attorney to help you negotiate a proper agreement for this situation.

Don't get me wrong. There are a lot of talented, honest producers who can spot raw talent and can produce a really great recording for you. Just beware and be cautious. Remember that a solid demo is only one piece of the puzzle. A brilliant two-song demo recording that costs you a few thousands dollars (or more) will *not* get you a record deal if you have not developed all of your talents first. Anyone trying to convince you otherwise is probably a lot more interested in their own pocketbooks than in your musical goals or interests.

Things You Can Do Today To Build Your Career
1) It's possible that another local artist who has enjoyed some success on a regional or national level would be willing to produce a few tracks for you. Look into that as an option.
2) Some colleges of music have very in-depth recording programs. It's possible to find a student who is willing to produce your record for free. Just remember that this person won't have as much experience as a professional producer. Be sure to listen to his or her previous work before committing to the arrangement.
3) Save your money and hire a professional producer for your entire full-length recording, or for a few tracks. Be sure to be clear about your budget from the get-go.

HOW THE PRODUCER GETS PAID

*U*sually, a producer is paid by the hour, by the number of master recordings completed, or a flat fee. In addition, the producer will probably ask for a royalty from the sale of the record. This means you will have to account to the producer and pay him or her regularly as you sell records, even if you are selling them yourself. All of these issues need to be agreed upon in a written contract. As always, I recommend that you consult with an entertainment attorney to provide guidance in drafting and/or negotiating this contract.

The producer's up-front fee will vary (from $250 to $10,000 per song), based on his or her experience and success, your level of success, how many songs you are recording, whether you are making a demo or a full-length recording, and if you are recording on your own or for a record label. If you are recording for a label, the fee can be influenced by whether the label is a local, national independent, or major label. Producers who create the original music to which artists simply add vocals cost more. The producer you select will depend on the type of recording you want to make and, naturally, on your budget.

Aside from a flat fee, the producer, like the artist, will receive a record sales royalty. This is usually a percentage of the sale price of a record, paid to the producer each time one of your records is sold. If the producer assists in writing or arranging your music, he or she will receive one more royalty—a "mechanical royalty," described below—which is paid by the record company for use of the song.

The sales royalty for a producer is usually 3%. So if your record sells for $16.98, the producer will receive 3% of that amount, or about $0.50, for each copy sold. However, this 3% (or "three points," as it is called in the record industry) is not an extra amount paid by the record company. In fact, it comes out of the artist's royalties. So if a record contract says you, the artist, are paid a royalty of 13% of the retail price for each record sold, you will actually get only 10%, or "ten points." The three points paid to the producer will be taken from your 13 royalty points.

This may not seem fair, but it is the way it works. Hopefully, knowing this hard fact in advance will help you make a better deal for yourself with the record label and keep you from giving out too many royalties to producers. Your entertainment attorney will know about this aspect of the record business and will be able to guide you.

The other royalty that can be paid to a producer is a "mechanical royalty," which is paid to a songwriter for the record company's right to record the song. If your producer helps to write or arrange a song on your record, the record company will pay the producer (and you, of course) for the right to record this song. If you are the sole songwriter and do not want your producer to share in your mechanical royalties, you should make this clear in any contract you make with the producer prior to going into the studio.

The mechanical royalty is based on U.S. copyright laws, which change from time to time. From January 1, 2004, through December 31, 2005, the mechanical royalty rate is 8.5 cents for each song on a record. A record company will negotiate to pay the songwriter(s) a lower rate, usually 75% of the current rate for each record sold. Under the current rate, the reduced amount would be approximately 6.4 cents per song. A producer who writes the music as, for example, many hip-hop producers do, would own half of the song and be entitled to one-half of the mechanical royalty. Therefore, the record company would pay 3.2 cents to the producer and pay the remaining 3.2 cents to the writer of the words, usually the artist. (The mechanical royalty rate will change to 9.1 cents in 2006.)

As you can imagine, this system can become complicated if you use several producers for your record. Therefore, before hiring a producer to do any work, consult with an entertainment attorney to determine the best way to approach a contract with the producer you select. Finally, you *must* have a written agreement with the producer—no matter what level you are at in your career—to make sure you protect your copyright ownership of the masters and your songs.

Things You Can Do Today To Build Your Career

1) Talk with various producers about their rates. Then do some math and figure out who will do the best job for the amount of money you're willing to spend. Per-song rates range from $250 to $10,000.

2) Read some sample recording contracts and understand the term "royalty" and "point." Decide if you and your band are willing to share points with the producer or if you need to find someone who is willing to work for an up-front fee only.

3) You must have a written agreement with your producer. A producer agreement can be downloaded at *MusicBusinessMadeSimple.com*. Remember not to sign anything until your entertainment attorney has reviewed or prepared the contract.

PART
FOUR

GETTING
A
RECORD
DEAL

Getting a Record Deal: An Overview

There are many approaches to establishing a relationship with a record label. Every artist, manager, producer, and entertainment attorney will vary in their approach, depending on past experience and success. But in all cases, development is the first and single most important step towards obtaining a record deal. Before you'll get anywhere with labels, you must be able to present yourself as an artist who has both talent and experience in recording and performing.

This presentation begins with a promotional package, or "promo pack," that includes a good-quality recording of songs, a brief artist biography and list of accomplishments, and a photo. This package will evolve and develop along with you, as you work toward the time when you present yourself to a record label. The promo pack is discussed in more detail in chapter 18, "Creating Your Promotional Package."

An honest, objective assessment of your talents and accomplishments will dictate the types of labels to which you send your package. Your manager, producer, or entertainment attorney can help you in this decision-making process. These professionals will also make sure your promo pack is complete and of sufficient quality. If they have record label contacts, ask them to send your promo pack to those companies on your behalf. Their knowledge of, and contacts within, the industry will help them evaluate your development, presentation, talents, and musical genre to determine which labels might be right for you. However, if they do not have some real relationship or contact with the labels you are approaching, there is no reason why you can't send the package yourself.

In this case, though, stick with independent labels, which are far more likely than major record companies to open and review what you send. If you are doing this on your own, an independent label is probably more appropriate for your level of development anyway. Generally, major record labels do not accept unsolicited packages (i.e., ones they did not request). So if you send your package to a major label just because you think they should have it, you'll receive it back in the mail.

Instead, save the postage and keep working on your creative development. If you have begun to enjoy some success—as demonstrated by publicity from your recordings, live performances, and/or independent record sales—and a label representative hears about you, he or she will contact you and ask for a promotional package. If things go well, the next step will be for him or her to come see you perform live.

In fact, before a label signs you, they always want to see your performance. If the label is in or near your city, a representative might come to your show at a local venue without your knowledge. If he or she is impressed with your live performance, the representative will usually ask you to perform a special show, to "showcase" your talents for label representatives. This topic is discussed in greater length in chapter 38, "Showcasing." This event may take place in your area, or in the city where the label is located. Most times, you will play in a club or other live music venue, but I have known some artists who actually had a showcase in the office of the record label.

If the decision makers at the label believe you are the kind of artist they want to sign, they will discuss entering into a contractual relationship. If you don't already have an entertainment attorney, this is definitely the time to hire one to represent you in any further discussions.

Things You Can Do Today To Build Your Career
1) Reassess your musical skills, your songs, your live performance, and your promotional package. What are your strengths? What are your weaknesses? Before approaching a label, work to correct those weaknesses.
2) Do some research and draw up a list of record labels that would make a good home for you. Make sure they work with your genre of music.
3) If you're asked to do a showcase, prepare for it as best as you can. Practice, practice, practice, and perfect your live set.

WHAT DOES A RECORD LABEL DO?

*I*f you're going to be in the music business, it will be helpful for you to understand the role of record labels, both within the industry and in your personal career. First, understand that a record label's sole function is to sell records. Except for the money a label invests in producing records, every dollar it spends has one purpose: To sell records, or, in industry lingo, "product." While there is a human factor to this equation (the artist), a record label is really no different from a company that sells soap or cereal. It will conduct marketing studies to determine the type(s) of consumers that will purchase your record. Then, the label will promote your record to get those consumers to buy it. I know it sounds cynical, but both you and the record you have worked so hard to create are just products—sources of income—to the record company.

Record companies will promote the sales of an artist's records through advertising in all media, such as magazines, radio, television, and the Internet. They may hire independent radio promoters to seek airplay of your songs. They will promote your product in record stores by paying for those posters you always see on the walls, and by having a copy of your record at a listening station or in special high-visibility areas in the store. The label's publicity department will send your record to magazines and newspapers, hoping to obtain a good review of your record or a story about you. The size of the label and its monetary resources will dictate the kinds and amount of promotion it is able to do.

Not surprisingly, smaller labels have smaller promotion budgets. Understand this when considering record labels, so you don't have a misconception about what a particular company can or cannot do for you. When talking to labels, ask how much they have to spend on promotion and advertising, and how they use these dollars for new and established artists. Assuming your first label is a small independent, expect no more than for them to produce your recording as well as they can, do minimal advertising and radio promotion, and provide you with records to sell at your live shows. This is completely acceptable for an artist early in his or her career.

The record company's job is to promote and sell your records, not to develop you as an artist. It is important to understand the difference. Most labels will not be interested until you have developed to the point where they can spend their time and money promoting your record, while you tour and make appearances to promote your record further. It always comes down to you selling records to make money for the label. A label's level of interest in signing you will depend on the amount of success you already have had in your career, your level of development, and your talent. They will not be interested in helping to advance your career (and, in fairness, they shouldn't be) unless it makes money for the company.

Record companies do not have staffs to groom you as an artist, so don't expect this. Your artistic development and career advancement are up to you and the professionals who work with you, such as your manager, entertainment attorney, booking agent, publishing company, voice and performance coaches, music teachers, etc. (See chapter 21, "Some Professionals You Will Need.") Even after you sign with a record label, you will continue to employ these professionals to continue to improve your skills as an artist and help you achieve your career goals.

You may come across people or labels, usually locally, who say they want to do it all for you. They will say they can provide coaching to help develop your skills and talents for live performance and recording. They may want to manage you and book your shows, and help you produce a record. While they may help you to produce a recording, it is important to look beyond their promises and find out about what they have done for other artists, and how much success they have had as a record label.

Companies that make these kinds of claims are usually production and development businesses that help artists to develop their talents for the purpose of obtaining a deal with some other record company. Or they are production and development companies that think they want to be record labels. It is fine to work with companies like this early in your development. Just be careful. *Before* entering into an agreement with them (or anyone), hire an entertainment attorney to help you negotiate appropriate terms, so both sides know what is expected of them.

Ultimately, you'll have the greatest chance of success if you are able to align yourself with a reputable record label that does a good job promoting you and selling your product. Your career will certainly benefit from these efforts, even if the label really is working only for its own best interest. If the record company is successful in promoting the sale of your record, they will be happy because they are making money. And you will be happy because these successes will increase your demand, notoriety, and income.

Things You Can Do Today To Build Your Career
1) Accept the fact that record companies do not develop raw talent. Development is your job. The record company is interested only in selling records. They want you to be the complete package when you approach them.
2) Record companies promote their artists via advertising and publicity. If you've got connections in the media, use them and help your label land reviews and other opportunities that will help sell records.
3) If you need additional artistic development, hire pros to help you: Vocal coach, media coach, etc.

START YOUR CAREER WITH 34 AN INDEPENDENT LABEL

*I*f you've begun to think it may be a while before you're ready for a major label… excellent! Chances are, you're correct. But don't despair. You have options. The most valuable of these is probably the independent, or "indie," label.

I cannot overstress the importance of independent labels. They influence the music industry by introducing new genres of music and by promoting new artists or those who may not have a "mainstream" style. Perhaps you've already noticed that a lot of the hottest, freshest music comes from indie labels. This is because independent record companies generally don't market to the masses, trying to sell millions of copies, as major labels do. Instead, they usually try to establish themselves as leaders within a specific musical niche, and then promote their artists/records to people who are interested in that type of music.

I believe musical artists should start their careers as early as possible, and that an indie label is the best place to begin. Independent labels will sign artists who are still developing and help them in many critical areas, especially in learning the recording process. The opportunity to "learn on the job" is the single most important reason to begin your career with an indie.

Another very important benefit of recording your first records with an independent label is that indies usually allow you more artistic freedom than major labels in deciding which songs you record and how you record them.

They will also give you some opportunity to find your musical "voice," develop a songwriting and performance style, etc. Major labels will expect you to have honed and perfected all of your artistic tools before they sign you.

Still, independent labels will notice you for the same reasons major labels will: You have developed your musical, performance, and writing skills; built an audience; recorded a few demos on your own; generated a little public and industry interest, or "buzz"; and sent a promo pack to the label. The difference is that indies often will not require the same level of development and perfection that major labels do.

There are independent labels all over the U.S. You can find contact and other information about them in a variety of music-industry resources. Check music magazines that cater to independent music, such as College Music Journal's *CMJ New Music Monthly*, or music-industry directories like *Recording Industry Sourcebook* and *Musician's Atlas*.

Begin your search for an independent label in your own backyard. Your experience with record labels will be a series of steps. Local independent labels can be a great first step. Why? Because these labels will know the music and the market in your area. They will know what resources are available to promote you in the local market (i.e., public-access radio stations, newspapers, and magazines—along with the people who work at these places). This is very helpful in making you known to local fans and consumers, who can purchase your records and come to see you perform.

No matter which labels you decide to contact, always remember to be professional in your approach. Small labels value a good first impression at least as much as the big ones do. Further, since indie labels are more likely to be interested in helping to develop your career, it pays to be professional and courteous.

How do you know when to approach independent labels? If you've started selling a few of your self-made cassettes or CDs, making a little money from your performances, and generally enjoying some success at the local and/or regional level, you can begin to think about working with a label. You've worked hard to get to this point, and you've proven that you and/or your group can generate income for a label by selling your records. It's time to let someone else spend a little money to record, market, and promote you and your record.

Sure, you could do all this yourself. In fact, you probably have been handling your career alone for some time. But why not let someone else use his or her resources to help? You just need to see this type of deal for what it really is. For example, you wouldn't ask your local indie label (which probably sells about 3,000 copies of each record it releases) to pay a large advance, agree to make a video, etc.

If you are a new artist, entering your first record deal with a local independent label for two records, you won't receive the same promotional support and dollars that you would get from a large independent or a major record company. The label simply can't afford it. Besides, you will have to prove your ability to make money for a label before a larger company will make a big investment in you. As the old cliché says, you have to "pay your dues." In this business, there are a lot of dues to pay.

You should expect no more from a small indie label than for them to produce your recording as well as they can on a minimal budget, do some local and regional advertising and radio promotion, and provide you with CDs to sell at your live shows. Just make sure you get the maximum benefit from this opportunity. If you understand what the contract will provide and how much it will help your career, you can make an informed decision about whether or not to enter into a short-term recording agreement. (Don't forget to have an attorney review the contract before you sign.)

It's pretty simple, really. You want someone else to pay for the production and manufacture of your records, and to promote you to a small area. You would have to do this yourself if a record company didn't do it for you. An independent label will not make you a star, and you shouldn't expect it to do this. Rather, appreciate indies for being a valuable development tool. They can assume some of the costs and responsibilities you have been taking on yourself, and maybe even give you a chance to make a little money. In the process, you will continue to grow as a musician and performer, and learn about the next steps that will advance your career in the music industry even further.

Things You Can Do Today To Build Your Career

1) Accept the fact that you may not get a major label deal at the start of your career. But you can get a good deal with an indie and spend some time there honing your craft. Use that opportunity wisely.

2) Research indie labels that release music of your genre. Send them your promotional pack. Continue to practice and improve your live set and your songwriting skills.

3) Treat everyone—and each potential deal—professionally. You never know when someone will move on to a new, higher profile position and remember you... for better or worse.

What to Look for in a Record Label

Most artists will never have record labels lining up to sign them. More than likely, only one label will be interested in signing you at any given point of your career. Nonetheless, you should sign with a label *only* if it is reputable, experienced, and knowledgeable about the music business. It's better to remain unsigned than to get trapped in a bad deal with a record company that can't (or won't) help advance your career.

A recording agreement does not guarantee success for your record. Your entertainment attorney will attempt to negotiate the best deal possible, but if the record company is not able or willing to deliver (i.e., produce a good record and then promote and sell it), it won't matter what the contract says. You'll be out of luck, and your music career will be stuck in neutral. This can happen even to established artists, and it can be very damaging when you are just beginning.

Not often, but sometimes, even if only one label shows interest, you might be better off not signing. Here are some basic things to consider before making that decision. Most of these concerns are more common when dealing with independent labels. However, they can apply to major labels, too.

First, make sure the record company has produced, released, and promoted records before yours. Be concerned if you'll be the label's first artist.

Every label has to start somewhere, but you don't want to be the guinea pig.

It's easy for a label to pay for a producer and studio time, and to get your album recorded. But you also want a label with knowledgeable, experienced people who know how to promote and advertise your record properly. Even if you have the greatest-sounding record of all time, no one will buy it if they don't know it exists. Promotion sells records. It's also the hardest job of a record company. Make sure a label is able to produce *and* promote your record.

Second, listen to other records put out by the label. Be sure they're making good-quality recordings, and that they produce the kind of music you perform. Unlike large labels, which can produce every style of music, from rock to country to R&B, most small labels don't have enough resources to put out more than one genre.

That's okay. When it comes to indies, the more diversified the label, the less likely it is they'll have expertise in your genre of music. In fact, you should seek out labels that strive to be experts at producing only one style of music (obviously, the label's focus needs to match up with your music).

These labels concentrate on finding the best producers and studios for their type of music. They know how to locate, work with, and promote artists who make that music and how to advertise specifically to those artists' audience(s). By creating a niche for themselves, they maximize the impact of their limited funding (and the success of their artists). Labels like SubPop, Rap-A-Lot, Blue Note, Rounder, and Alligator are great examples of small companies having a huge influence on their corner of the music industry.

Third, check out the label's reputation to make sure it's a company with which you want to sign. You can do this by talking to people in the industry—especially artists—who deal with the label. Ask for their opinions. Don't be surprised or discouraged if you get some negative responses. People may be disgruntled because they entered into bad record deals, or because they relied too heavily on the label for their success.

But if you get a lot of bad feedback, it may be indicative of legitimate problems at the label. Listen and look at the quality of the label's releases. Ask people if the label has solid distribution, marketing, and promotional abilities. Also ask what they like best and least about the label. Understand that the first artists signed by smaller labels may have been experimental guinea pigs. Mistakes were probably made, and everything might not have gone smoothly. Chances are, the label has gained experience and knowledge since then. You're likely to get a more positive response, and a more accurate view of current operations, from artists who have worked with the label more recently.

Fourth, look to see if the label has a staff to take care of administration, or if it's just one person doing everything. Naturally, a small label will have fewer resources, including personnel. But one individual cannot do it all. The label should have at least a few people to coordinate marketing and promotion for your record. And if they don't have their own personnel, they should be using independent promoters to fulfill this critical function.

Finally, no matter how big the label is, discuss their goals and plans for you to determine if they understand how to promote and market your music. If you already have developed a fan base and have achieved some successes—through previous recordings, radio airplay, regional touring, and fan support—the label should listen to you and be willing to work with you to build upon those successes. Also discuss your artistic goals with the label to see if they understand and support you as an artist.

This information does not always come easily. You will have to do your homework, communicate with the label, and talk to people who deal with the label. It takes some work, but it can save you a lot of heartache, time, and money later on. You'll want to follow the same process whether signing with a tiny label, a major independent, or an international record company. Just because a label is successful does not mean they know how to market your record or that they share your career goals. In any case, your "background check" will provide information to help you decide whether or not to sign with a specific record company.

Things You Can Do Today To Build Your Career
1) Find out what other artists the label has released and listen to their CDs.
2) Before signing any record deal agreement, make sure the label can follow up on its promises. Talk with artists on the label (and those who were in the past). Does the label hold up its end of the bargain in terms of distribution and promotion?
3) Make sure the label has a staff or other personnel that can market and promote your records.

WHAT ARE THEY 36 LOOKING FOR?

So what are record labels looking for? The more experience I gain in this business, the more confident I feel in saying, "Your guess is as good as mine." No one, including me, can say what kinds of artists the record labels are going to sign tomorrow, or what music the labels will market to commercial radio and the consumer as "pop." However, I can give you an idea of the general qualities many labels look for in the artists they sign. The two main things a label seeks are (1) music that will appeal to an identifiable market, and (2) artists who can deliver that music.

However, there is no way to know from year to year (or even month to month) what type(s) of music or artists major labels will sign, or what the labels will decide is right for the "pop" markets of people between the ages of 13 and 19. Understand that pop music of today may not be popular tomorrow. In fact, there's a very good chance it won't be. So it's a waste of time to set your development path based on what is popular today. The only way that would work is if you are already a fully developed artist who can step right in and begin to perform today's "pop" music as soon as the label signs you and begins to market your music.

If your music is clearly part of a specific market, like country, Americana, jazz, blues, classical, or hip-hop (to name a few), it will be fairly easy to identify labels that might want to sign you. But even these genres change over time. The country music on today's commercial stations is very different from the country music of 30, 40, or 50 years ago. There is still a large market for country music, but the music has changed over generations. These changes occur in all genres over time, either because labels think the market has shifted, or because several innovative new artists have influenced that change.

If your music does not have a "commercial" radio appeal or an identifiable market, it may be more difficult to find a record label that knows how to work with you. This definitely does not mean you should change your music to meet the market, or that you will be limited in your innovation, creativity, or performance. Even if you can't categorize your music, you can have a great career, get signed, and sell records. There will just be fewer labels releasing, marketing, and selling the type of music you make, so it may take a little longer to find a record deal.

You may think your music is really innovative and cool (and it may be), but a record label has to be able to identify a market for your records. Whether you're with an independent or major label, it's always going to be about marketing. Remember, a record label's sole purpose is to sell records and make money. If they can't identify your audience, they can't sell your records. Therefore, there's no reason for them to sign you. Then again, you really don't want to be on a label—even if they just love your music—if they don't know how to sell it.

Once you have selected some labels that might match up with your musical style, you need to show them you know what you're doing. Of course, they seek artists who can sing and/or play an instrument, but that's not enough. To be considered for a record deal, you also need solid songs, a professional approach, and great performance skills, regardless of the type of music you perform.

Because record labels are always looking for new, quality product to sell to their customers, it helps if you are original, creative, talented, and marketable. Part of your job as a developing artist is to make yourself marketable before you begin to contact record labels. You do this by writing songs and rehearsing, performing, recording, and releasing records, all with the goal of building a fan base.

You have to demonstrate that on your own (or with the help of an independent label), you have built an audience who like what you do and are willing to buy your records and pay to see you perform. You want to show labels that, with a little help, you can do all this on a grander scale. Which, of course, will make money for the label. Remember, although A&R (artists and repertoire) representatives may look for artists they like, record companies are in the business of promoting artists only to the point that the artists put money in the labels' pockets.

Prospective labels will also examine the professional personnel with whom you have aligned yourself. Local independent labels will not necessarily require you to have management or a booking agent, but this is an important consideration with larger independent and major labels. It is your responsibility, not the label's, to build your professional team. You must do this before you present your package to most record labels (certainly, larger indies and major labels).

Labels need to know that if they release your record, you have personnel in place to help coordinate the administrative and promotional efforts of that release. Moreover, the members of your team need to show they know what they're doing and that they can be successful in their roles. I'm not exaggerating when I say, sometimes, the skills and experience of your team can be the deciding factor in whether or not a label chooses to work with you.

Finally, a label wants professionalism and a good first impression. Even if it turns out you're not right for a particular label at a given time, your professional approach and excellent presentation might make you a friend or two along the way. Maybe your A&R contact will keep an eye on your developing career. Maybe he or she will put in a good word for you every once in a while, as label priorities change. Or maybe that contact will move to another label that will be interested in you right now. You never know.

It all starts with a good first impression. This is why you don't go running from your garage recording session to the post office to send your first-ever demo tape to Warner Bros. It is why inexperienced artists and managers should not call Sony Music and expect to get the time of day. It's a waste of your time and theirs, and a serious mistake for you.

Instead, have reputable managers, producers, and entertainment attorneys evaluate your promotional package and level of development. Have them present you to record labels as a serious, developed artist with the ability to sell lots of records. With this professional approach, you can show labels they have found what they're looking for, or at least, that you are worthy of their attention and respect.

Things You Can Do Today To Build Your Career

1) Don't try to be a carbon-copy of an artist that is popular today. Focus on the music you like to create and do it. An audience will follow.

2) If your music is not "commercial," find other outlets that will lead to a fan base: Play music festivals that focus on your genre, start an e-newsletter devoted to that genre, and/or cross-promote your music with other like-minded artists.

3) Let prospective record labels know that you already have a following and the resources to reach your audience once a deal is signed.

GETTING 37 NOTICED

So how do you introduce yourself to the music industry? Well, you start by developing your playing and songwriting skills, perfecting your live performance, adopting a professional attitude, and preparing the best promotional package, or "promo pack," possible.

After that, you can get a record label's attention in two ways. First, they might hear about you through the industry grapevine because of the buzz you're creating with record sales, radio airplay, great live performances, media coverage, or all of the above. You can be doing all this while signed to a smaller label or working independently. The other way to get noticed is to send your promo pack to record labels' A&R departments, in a process known as "shopping" yourself.

Major record labels receive hundreds of promo packs each week. The challenge is to set yourself apart and capture the label's interest. The promo pack should demonstrate your talents, originality, professionalism, and successes related to quality of recordings, record sales, live performance, and radio airplay. I explain the promo pack in detail in chapter 18, "Creating Your Promotional Package." Just remember, while it is very important to have a strong, eye-catching promo pack, its purpose is to exemplify your successes as an artist. This should always be your main focus.

After sending your promo pack, do not expect a call from the label's A&R department, saying they want to sign you immediately. Be prepared for rejection and indifference. You may send your promo pack to every label on the planet and not get a single response. Remember, a record label has no responsibility to do anything beyond throwing your package in the trash. As a courtesy, some labels may send an official rejection letter before they throw your package in the trash. Some may simply return your package unopened.

Don't take this personally; it's just how this business works sometimes. It doesn't mean your music is bad, or that you aren't worthy of a record deal. There are a thousand reasons why any given label might not want to sign an artist, and a lot of those reasons have nothing to do with the artist's talent or the quality of the music. The fact is most people looking for a record deal get turned down. You just have to keep trying.

If you do get a personal response from a label, consider yourself one of the lucky few. The label might say that your material is good, but they are not seeking new talent at this time, or that your music is not what they are looking for. This response may be a handwritten note or a telephone call.

In any case, a personal response means you have been noticed. As your career continues to progress, you should update the person at the label who responded to your promo pack. As you make new recordings or have other successes you should send the recordings or the latest news to the label. Don't contact the label every week (they will lose interest quickly if you do), but only when you have something really important to share.

If the label representative begins to see significant development and success from you, he or she may come to see your performance. In fact, you may have A&R representatives following your career as you continue to progress in your career. You may not even know they are there, but when/if the time is right, they'll contact you to discuss the next steps.

Things You Can Do Today To Build Your Career

1) Create "buzz" about your music. Perform as often as you can, promote your music aggressively, and be professional at all times. You never know who'll turn up at a gig or who will end up with your promo pack.

2) Send your promo pack to influential music-industry individuals. Keep in touch with those who have offered positive encouragement, if not a record deal. Don't bombard them with correspondence, but do stay in contact.

3) Be prepared for an A&R scout to show up at one of your gigs. Don't let this throw you. Just put your heart into the performance and do the best you can.

SHOWCASING

*I*f a label is interested after reviewing your promo pack and accomplishments, they will ask you to "showcase," or perform live for a label representative. Obviously, this will be one of the most important performances of your career, so it is critical to have developed and perfected your
live show well before it occurs. Experienced managers, producers, or attorneys will not even begin to send out your promo package or shop you to
labels until your live performance is ready for a showcase.

If you have a great performance the first time a label sees you, they
probably will want to see you perform several more times before making a
decision about you. They may also have their colleagues from the label
come to your shows and listen to your recordings. Their goal is to determine
your consistency as a live performing artist, and to compare your sound
onstage to the sound on your recordings.

You can spend a lot of money with a brilliant producer to create a great-
sounding studio recording. But the label will not be interested for long if
you can't match that sound in your live show, and if your performance is
not on a level with other artists on the label.

To impress the label, your live performance should be better than they
expect from your recordings. The best way to prepare for this opportunity
is to rehearse and perform over and over. Pay special attention to perfecting
your "A" set, as I describe in chapter 14, "A Formula for Performing." This

is the day you have been working for, the moment when all the practice, crummy gigs, low pay, and lugging your gear from one dive to another can pay off. Prepare and perform as if your career depended on this show. It might.

There are different ways to showcase. The best situation is to showcase in a familiar venue in your hometown, with the soundman of your choice, in front of all your screaming fans. This helps your performance because you know the sound will be good and you can feed off the energy of your fans to perform a good show.

Unfortunately, some labels will not be able or willing to travel to see you, so you will have to go to them. It may be difficult to obtain a show outside your regular performing area, but most labels have contacts at clubs in their areas. They can usually help you book a show.

It can be a big challenge to play in a new place, especially with so much at stake. You do not know the sound or feel of the venue, your fans will not be there, and, most of all, you will be at the mercy of a soundman who has never heard you before. Furthermore, you may have a limited time to perform, so you'll have to adapt your set to fit the time allotted.

You'll experience these same difficulties if you perform at a music festival, such as South by Southwest in Austin, Texas, or CMJ Music Marathon in New York City. But if this is your only chance to showcase for a label representative, you have to step up, show your professionalism, and do your best. If you're really good, the representative may choose to come see you in your hometown next time.

Things You Can Do Today To Build Your Career
1) Even if you're invited to "showcase" for a label, you'll probably have to play for them several times. Each performance must be perfect. Get ready for this by practicing as often as possible.
2) If you do showcase, try to do it in your hometown and in a familiar venue. Invite all your fans and make sure they are pumped for the event. The more comfortable you feel, the better you'll play. Feed off your audience's energy!
3) Try to land a showcase spot at a music conference. The most popular are South by Southwest and CMJ Music Marathon.

SIGNING THE CONTRACT 39

*H*opefully, the label will eventually decide to speak with you about entering into a relationship. At that time, you *must* have an entertainment attorney to consult with and to represent you in any contract negotiations. It's good to establish a relationship with an attorney before this moment so you will have time to discuss your plan of action and make sure the attorney understands what you want and need from a record contract. This helps you obtain the best deal possible.

If you and the label are satisfied with each other and decide to enter into an agreement, the label will prepare either a deal memo, a short form of the recording agreement, or the actual recording agreement for review by you and your entertainment attorney. The main terms of the agreement, such as the number of records you will record, your basic royalty rate, and the amount of your recording advance, may have been negotiated in advance by your manager or attorney and included in the document.

It is very important to have an entertainment attorney involved from the start of this process, *before* you sign anything, so you do not end up accidentally agreeing to terms that you do not understand or don't want. Once you sign, your attorney will not be able to persuade the label to change terms to which you already have agreed.

Your attorney will review the deal memo, short form, or long-form contract and explain it to you. At that time, you will tell the attorney what your expectations are and what you want to have included in, or deleted from, the contract. Your attorney will explain which of your requests are realistic and which (if any) are not. After you and your attorney have agreed about what the contract should say, your attorney will enter into negotiations with the record company to obtain a final contract that is reasonable and fair, based on your level of success and how badly the label wants you.

The attorney is your advocate, but he or she may not be able to get everything you want from the record label. His or her job is to negotiate a legally binding agreement that you and the label find acceptable. Understand that the contract negotiations can take a long time. For major labels, it can take six months or longer, based on the schedules of the attorneys on both sides, as well as your availability and the record label's ability to meet with you and/or your attorney when necessary. But through negotiation and compromise, a deal will be reached and you will sign a contract to record for the label. Congratulations. Your career has just moved to the next level.

Things You Can Do Today To Build Your Career

1) If you don't already have an entertainment attorney, start looking for one now. You must have a lawyer review any record deal before you sign. A sample recording agreement can be downloaded at *MusicBusinessMadeSimple.com*.
2) The contract process can be a slow one. Don't be worried by this. Take your time and make sure your attorney negotiates the best deal possible.
3) Realize that with a signed contract, your work as an artist is just beginning. Start working even harder!

A FINAL WORD OF ENCOURAGEMENT 40

Throughout this book, I emphasize the importance of independent labels to your development. Of course, a major-label contract can be in your goals, but it should not be your first goal. Never lose sight of your primary objective: To be a successful artist based on what you do. There will be many pathways by which you can reach that objective. Some will include a major label and some will not. But a major-label record deal is not the only path to success in this industry.

I believe artists should approach their development in a way that will allow them to have long-lasting careers in the music business. Musicians I know who have had long careers share the philosophy that they are artists first, and that they will be artists regardless of whether they have a record deal or not. These artists have started on smaller labels, honing their skills and building a foundation through record sales, radio airplay, and touring. Eventually, their hard work and achievements got them noticed by major labels.

But that is not the main goal. They don't measure success by the label they're on, and you shouldn't either. For these people, success means being a musical artist, performing the music they love, and selling records at their shows and through local/regional distribution, either on their own or with the aid of a record label. They rely upon their live performances and consistent radio airplay on non-commercial radio stations to build a fan base that buys their records and pays to see them perform. In fact, this is how most artists are able to have long careers in the music business.

It's a model that can work for you, too. Hard work, a solid plan, and love of your art can help you sustain a career in this industry. Eventually, if you are successful as an artist, the majors will find you, and the deal will be on your terms, not theirs.

You will not get a record deal after a chance encounter with an A&R representative at the local record store. Neither will you be signed based solely on a demo tape, no matter how great it is. Good luck and a good recording are only two of many elements needed to be signed by a label.

Forget about the exceptions, the *American Idol* miracles, and the "one-hit-wonders." Instead, accept the rule that development is the key, and that development takes time. The earlier you begin, the sooner you will begin to advance your music career and possibly get noticed by a record label.

As I state in the introduction, luck is when preparation meets opportunity. If you prepare yourself by developing your musical abilities, writing and recording songs, playing live as often as possible, and constantly improving your performance skills, opportunities will arise. The harder you work, the more opportunities you will have to get noticed by a record label. So get started and make it happen.

Resources

Magazines for Musicians

Acoustic Guitar
A magazine devoted to guitarists who have gone acoustic.
(800) 827-6837
www.acousticguitar.com

Alternative Press
The editors cover everything with an eye toward alternative music and culture.
(800) 339-2675 x115
www.altpress.com

American Songwriter
The magazine reports on the craft and business of songwriting.
(800) 739-8712
www.americansongwriter.com

Bass Player
One of the only magazines for bass players.
(800) 234-1831
www.bassplayer.com

Billboard
This is the industry tip sheet for musicians and record-company executives. A must-read.
(800) 745-8922
www.billboard.com

Canadian Musician
Canada's magazine for professional and amateur musicians.
(877) RING-NWC
www.canadianmusician.com

CMJ New Music
For new music, there's no better resource.
(917) 606-1908 Ext. 248
www.cmj.com

Country Weekly
For fans and musicians alike, *Country Weekly* focuses on country and Americana music.
(877) 566-5832
www.countryweekly.com

Electronic Musician
Great publication for electronic musicians and those interested in the recording arts.
(800) 245-2737
www.electronicmusician.com

Guitar One Magazine
A must-read for guitarists.
(212) 561-3000
www.guitaronemag.com

Guitar Player
A must-read for guitarists.
(800) 289-9839.
www.guitarplayer.com

Keyboard
The magazine for keyboard aficionados.
(800) 289-9919
www.keyboardmag.com

Mix
A magazine for those interested in professional recording and production.
(800) 532-8190
www.mixonline.com

Modern Drummer
Well-respected magazine for drummers.
(800) 551-3786
www.moderndrummer.com

Performing Songwriter
This magazine discusses songwriting and the business of making music.
(800) 883-7664
www.performingsongwriter.com

Remix
Remix is designed for those interested in underground music production and DJ performance.
(800) 275-1989
www.remixmag.com

Sing Out!
Sing Out!'s mission is to preserve and support the cultural diversity and heritage of all traditional and contemporary folk music.
(888) SING-OUT
www.singout.org

RESOURCE DIRECTORIES

The Indie Bible by David Wimble
www.indiebible.com

Musician's Atlas
www.musiciansatlas.com

Recording Industry Sourcebook
www.artistpro.com

MUSIC-BUSINESS BOOKS

The Billboard Guide to Music Publicity by Jim Pettigrew

The Mansion on the Hill: Dylan, Young, Geffen, Springsteen, and the Head-On Collision of Rock and Commerce by Fred Goodman

Music, Money, and Success: The Insider's Guide to Making Money in the Music Industry by Jeffrey Brabec and Todd Brabec

They Fought the Law: Rock Music Goes to Court by Stan Soocher

MUSICIAN BIOGRAPHIES

Dave Grohl: Foo Fighters, Nirvana & Other Misadventures by Martin James

I, Me, Mine by George Harrison and Derek Taylor

Rolling Stones: Off the Record by Mark Paytress

Ryan Adams by Michael Heatley

Shakey: Neil Young's Biography by Jimmy McDonough

That's Alright, Elvis: The Untold Story of Elvis' First Guitarist and Manager, Scotty Moore by Scotty Moore with James Dickerson

MUSIC-TECHNIQUE BOOKS

The Little Book of Tips & Tricks for Guitar: The Complete Guide to Techniques, Soloing, Rhythm, and Styles by Music Sales

Writing Music for Hit Songs by Jai Josefs

MUSIC / RECORDING BOOKS FOR BEGINNERS

Producing Your Own CDs: A Handbook by Christian W. Huber

Quick Start: Home Recording by Ingo Raven

Quick Start: CD Burning by Paul Sellars

Quick Start: Audio Mastering by Craig Anderton

MUSIC CONFERENCES

Atlantis Music Conference
Held in Atlanta, Georgia in July
www.atlantismusic.com

Billboard Dance Music Summit
Location and date to be announced
www.billboardevents.com

Billboard R&B Hip Hop Conference & Awards
Location and date to be announced
www.billboardevents.com

Billboard Latin Music Conference & Awards
Location and date to be announced
www.billboardevents.com

CMJ Music Marathon
Held in New York City in October
www.cmj.com/marathon

Independent Music Conference
Held in Philadelphia in August
www.indiemusicon.com

Nashville New Music Conference
Held in Nashville in September
www.2nmc.com

NEMO Music Conference
Held in Boston in September
www.nemoboston.com

North by Northwest
Held in Seattle in September
www.nxnw.com

South by Southwest
Held in Austin, Texas, in March
www.sxsw.com

MUSIC-BUSINESS CONTRACTS

MusicContracts.com

MUSIC PUBLICITY

Entertainment Publicists Professional Society
www.eppsonline.org

PRINTERS

Printing For Less
High-quality, low-cost, four-color printing of presentation folders, business cards, one-sheets, postcards, flyers, etc.
The official sponsor of Music Business Made Simple *and the company who created promo packs for this book.*
www.printingforless.com

Modern Postcard
Good prices on four-color printing of postcards and greeting cards.
www.modernpostcard.com

PERFORMANCE RIGHTS ORGANIZATIONS

ASCAP (American Society of Composers, Authors, and Publishers)
(212) 621-6000
www.ascap.com

BMI (Broadcast Music, Inc.)
(212) 586-2000
www.bmi.com

SESAC (Society of European Stage Authors and Composers)
(615) 320-0055
www.sesac.com

THE MUSICIAN'S SOURCE
For High-Quality, Low-Cost
Four-Color Printing

CD Covers • Presentation Folders
Posters • Postcards • Business Cards
Greeting Cards • Bookmarks • Newsletters
Stationery • Brochures

Full-color printing of ALL digital file formats! Now you can get professional full-color printing of any Mac or PC file, including Quark, Publisher, Pagemaker, CorelDRAW! and all popular file formats with instant pricing, online ordering and proofing, and browser-based file uploading. For professional-quality printed pieces, including CD covers, posters, postcards, newsletters, brochures, mailers, and business cards, there is no substitute for true four-color-process lithography on glossy paper, printed on Heidelberg printing presses.

http://www.printingforless.com
info@printingforless.com
1-800-930-6040

INDEX